PREFACE

THE INTENDED AUDIENCE

It is tempting to describe this book as being about the beginnings of philosophy in ancient Greece. That description, however, would be misleading in an important way. For in fact the book is an account of those first philosophers *written for a specific audience*.

That audience can be identified quite easily. Every college and university philosophy department in the United States offers a course in Greek philosophy (or ancient philosophy). Typically, that course is the first of a sequence in the history of philosophy. Philosophy majors are normally required to take the entire sequence. Very often a considerable number of nonmajors enroll in such a course, since it frequently satisfies some general education requirement. Those students, whatever their intentions about future studies, overwhelmingly have little, if any, prior background in philosophy. In other words, the course in Greek philosophy is very much an introductory course.

That is the audience to whom this book is addressed. This book was designed to be used in a course composed of such students.

STRUCTURAL LIMITATIONS

The students in those courses in Greek philosophy share other characteristics that need to be taken into account when developing a text for them. For instance, they tend to know little of the history of civilization that gave rise to Western philosophy. However, the second major fact about those courses has to do not with the nature of the audience but with the structure of the course itself. In it, an instructor is expected to treat the Pre-Socratics, the Sophists, Socrates, Plato, Aristotle, and often Hellenistic philosophy too. All that material is to be discussed with appropriate intellectual rigor in the sumptuous period of a ten- to fifteen-week term.

Instructors know that this task is nearly impossible. In practice, every-thing gets squeezed and some material is omitted. To do proper justice to the major figures—say, Socrates, Plato, and Aristotle—the later and earlier periods are normally most radically trimmed or altogether axed.

ON TAILORING THE BOOK

This book has been designed for use in courses with objectives and audi-ences as just described. Of course, it may well be helpful, even stimulating, to other people in other circumstances. Yet that was not the intent with which I wrote the book. It is important here, in this preface, to note *how* the book has been tailored to that special set of circumstances. First, let me consider the structural issues.

If significant amounts of time are to be devoted to the central later figures, then there cannot be many classroom periods given over to the Pre-Socratics. Consequently, a usable text about the early Greek thinkers must be neither too long nor itself the object of extensive classroom exegesis. Hence I have aimed to produce a text that is brief, efficient, and clear. Assignments of moderate length will enable students to read it in three weeks. Lectures during those weeks can be used to expand on and discuss the material contained in the text. The aim of the writing project has been to provide time for a lecturer to engage in *those* activities, rather than to have to spend classroom time explaining the basic doctrines or the text itself.

To achieve that brevity, two things needed to be done: (1) to write eco-nomically yet clearly, and (even more important in achieving brevity than crispness and clarity of style) (2) to refrain from saying everything that *could* be said. Two types of subject matter in particular have been omitted here. One of those is the canvas of scholarly interpretations. Although beginning students need to know, both in general and with respect to particular theses, that scholars disagree widely and continuously about how to interpret the views of the Pre-Socratic philosophers, such students can safely be spared the details and even the outlines of that infighting. Their ability to grasp the bare contours of the philosophical material is impaired by plunges into the murky water of scholarship. Needing to omit something to make the book short enough, I relinquished an account of those disputes.

Secondly, the course for which this book is designed is a philosophy course. Yet the Pre-Socratics were also the first figures in the scientific tradi-tion. Again, introductory students must know that both Western science and philosophy derived from these ancient Greek thinkers. Nonetheless, if stu-dents are to grasp the story, they must not be burdened with the details of that early science. A student can learn those matters elsewhere—in fact, instructors can add that material in lecture if that is how they choose to spend the connected classroom time. A considerable saving of space and

BEGINNING WITH THE PRE-SOCRATICS

Second Edition

Merrill Ring
California State University, Fullerton

Mayfield Publishing Company
Mountain View, California
London • Toronto

Library of Congress Cataloging-in-Publication Data

Ring, Merrill.
  Beginning with the pre-Socratics / Merrill Ring. —2nd ed.
    p.   cm.
  Includes bibliographical references and index.
  ISBN 0-7674-1338-5
  1. Pre-Socratic philosophers. I. Title.
B187.5.R55   1999
182—dc21
                                                              99-21502
                                                              CIP

Manufactured in the United States of America

10   9   8   7   6   5   4   3   2

Mayfield Publishing Company
1280 Villa Street
Mountain View, CA 94041

Sponsoring editor, Kenneth King; production editor, Heather Collins; manuscript editor, Darlene Bledsoe; design manager, Jeanne Schreiber; text and cover designer, Linda M. Robertson; art editor, Robin Mouat; manufacturing manager, Randy Hurst. The text was set in 10/12 New Baskerville by Archetype Book Composition and printed on acid-free 50# Finch Opaque by Malloy Lithographing, Inc.

Cover image: PhotoDisc, Inc. 1999.

Chapter 1: pp. 7, 8, 10, M. I. Finley, *Early Greece* (New York: W. W. Norton & Company, 1970). Reprinted by permission of the publisher. Chapter 2: p. 14, from Hesiod's *Theogony,* translated by Richmond Lattimore. Copyright © 1959 by The University of Michigan. Reprinted by permission of The University of Michigan Press. Chapter 3: p. 26; Chapter 5: pp. 40, 44, 48; Chapter 6: p. 70; and Chapter 10: p. 143, W. K. C. Guthrie, *History of Greek Philosophy*, Volumes 1 and 2 (Cambridge University Press, Cambridge: 1962 and 1965). Reprinted by permission of the publisher.

time has been accomplished by omitting what would be counted as clearly scientific rather than philosophical problems (such as the explanation of earthquakes).

To have noted those two special omissions is not to say that *all else* has been discussed—the general principle of producing a brief book has made that impossible. Consequently, some topics of genuine philosophical interest have had to be omitted.

ON BEING HELPFUL TO THE AUDIENCE

This book was written not only in light of the time constraint on its use but also with the needs of the student audience in mind. There is, for example, a (brief) chapter on the history of ancient Greece, to enable students to locate the origin of philosophy in a historical context. When difficult names are introduced, a pronunciation is indicated to preclude stumbling or embarrassing guesses. There are discussions, even chapters, not often found in scholarly works about the Pre-Socratics; those have been included precisely because the readers are expected to be philosophy students, albeit at an introductory level. More commonly, I have included maps and (restrained) bibliographies.

Because the text is to be used in a course leading up through Plato and Aristotle, I have attempted to make some forward-looking connections from the Pre-Socratics to later philosophy. (The history of Greece is carried up to the Hellenistic period for the same reason.)

Lastly, the translations are my own, owing much to previous translators and current friends. However, in line with the general aims of the book, I have attempted to make those translations readable, sometimes with (modest) violation of the canons of literal accuracy.

CHANGES TO THIS EDITION

Reviewers have recommended that the book is most useful at its original length; therefore, all changes have been small. The most notable change, in light of a sensible recommendation by reviewers, is that the discussion of Melissus be eliminated. I have corrected two historical mistakes, shifted one discussion from late in the chapter on Miletus to the beginning of the chapter, and improved the text on a modest number of points. Someone who has been teaching the book will have to make only small alterations in practice to employ this new edition.

STYLE

It is wholly proper to be suspicious of an author who says, as I just have, that the aim was to write a clear and efficient text. Normally, such an aim would mean that the book had been rubbed clear of all traces of a human mind at work. In contemporary parlance, texts are usually "dumbed down"—written so that in both style and substance they are mush.

I aimed instead at writing with clarity and brevity for an introductory audience, without sacrificing linguistic and intellectual style. If all went as planned, the intended reader will have to *think* while reading but will not have to wallow in intellectual and verbal muck.

I did not intend to be original in what I had to say about the various Pre-Socratic philosophers, preferring my innovations to be those already discussed. For one thing, I wanted to exhibit my debt to those commentators from whom I have learned and to encourage readers to look into those writings. Hence, not only have I included bibliographies, but I also quote from those other authors when they have made a point so well that I could not hope to improve on it.

Even more, the object was not to present interpretations of the Pre-Socratics' views that exhibited my idiosyncracies. Nonetheless, as I worked, bits and pieces sprouted here that do not show up in standard interpretations. And the core of what I say about Parmenides is not found elsewhere.

THANKS

Of the considerable number of people who have been helpful with this project, I would especially like to acknowledge three. Peter Dill and David Depew encouraged me to be serious about writing this book, and Mary Depew has always been available on those frequent occasions when I needed to discuss how to translate something. Also, I am grateful to those who reviewed the manuscript and offered suggestions for improvement: Scott G. Schreiber, St. Norbert College; Anthony P. Roark, University of Washington; and Earle J. Coleman, Virginia Commonwealth University.

In the first edition, I should have included one more name: Alex Sesonske, who long ago started me thinking about early Greek philosophy. Here I need add two more appreciations: for correcting historical mistakes occurring in the first edition I thank Professor Stephen Glass, Classics, Pitzer College, and Professor James Santucci, Linguistics and Religious Studies, California State University, Fullerton.

CONTENTS

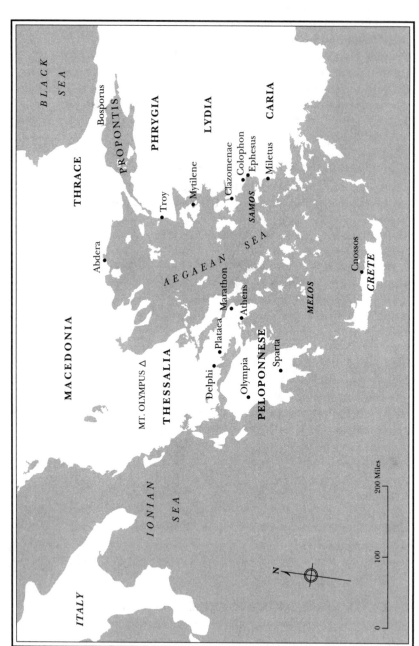

THE AEGEAN

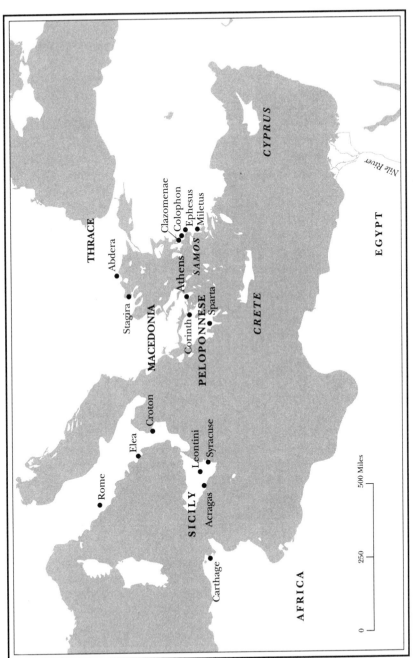

EASTERN MEDITERRANEAN

THRACE

Abdera

Stagira

MACEDONIA

Clazomenae
Colophon
Ephesus
Miletus

Athens

SAMOS

Corinth

PELOPONNESE

Sparta

Croton

Elea

Leontini

Syracuse

Rome

SICILY

Acragas

Carthage

CRETE

CYPRUS

Nile River

EGYPT

AFRICA

0   250   500 Miles

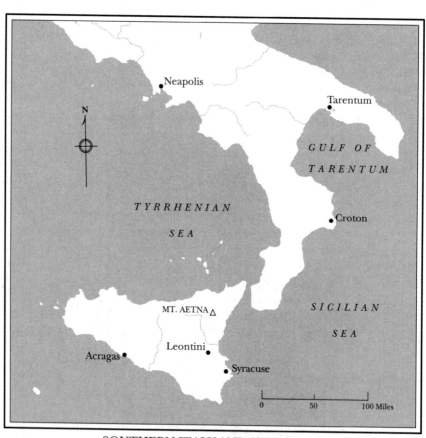

SOUTHERN ITALY AND SICILY

INTRODUCTION: STUDYING THE PRE-SOCRATICS

Although I am assuming that most readers of this book are new to philosophy, I shall not try to do what may seem desirable in view of that situation: namely, to offer some account of what philosophy is. Philosophy has been, and is, many sorts of things (which is not to say that it has been, and can be, anything and everything). Any formula or definition of it would, among other failings, misrepresent that diversity.

One way, though not the only way, to begin learning about philosophy is through its history. Like all fields of study, philosophy has not always existed, nor has it always been as it is now. Moreover, current philosophical ideas and problems are, for a very large part, the outcome of a long historical development. To see ideas coming into being and developing, to observe outlooks and problems shifting, significantly helps in making sense of why philosophy is what it is.

We have an additional reason for studying the history of philosophy. One can learn about and even engage in the practice of, say, chemistry with only the most rudimentary knowledge of its history. Chemistry and the sciences in general, although they too have evolved to be what they are now, are not taught and practiced as historical disciplines. Philosophy is different: philosophers are expected to know a good deal of their past. And that knowledge is not to be thought of as boring and irrelevant family history. Rather, an important part of *doing* philosophy is thinking about the questions asked, and the solutions offered, by one's philosophical ancestors. Hence, when students learn of philosophy's past, they are learning also of its present, learning what philosophical problems are and how to think about them.

Incidentally, notice that in the preceding discussion, I have implicitly put some restrictions on what is to be thought of as philosophy. Most obviously, I am taking philosophy as a discipline, an area of intellectual inquiry. It is something that can be studied, something with a past and with problems for which solutions can be presented and defended. Philosophy may be more than that, but it is at least that.

BEGINNING WITH THE PRE-SOCRATICS

The group of thinkers who are counted as first in the Western philosophical tradition were Greeks living from about 600 to 400 B.C.E. We call them the Pre-Socratics. That was not, of course, how they referred to themselves nor did they all live and work before Socrates. But the change that came over philosophy with Socrates was so great that we today use his name to set off his intellectual concerns from a prior and very different set of philosophical interests. Thus, to begin the study of philosophy at its beginning is to learn about the Pre-Socratics.

SOURCES OF OUR KNOWLEDGE

Every student of the Pre-Socratics needs to know at the outset that our knowledge of their thought is filled with difficulties. We do not possess one single complete manuscript from those thinkers, and most of what we have is considerably less than a full manuscript. Hence, all that we know about them comes from later authors. This second-hand information divides into two types: (1) *quotations* from otherwise lost Pre-Socratic manuscripts that have been preserved in the texts of later authors (these materials are usually spoken of as *fragments*), and (2) *reports,* by those later authors, of what the Pre-Socratics said (usually called *testimony*).

Scholars have to assess the reliability of the preserved material, even the purported quotations, for us to have any trustworthy information. And of course such scholars can and do differ in their assessment, and so disputes occur as to whether So-and-So really said such-and-such. Nor is that the end of the matter. Even if the authenticity of a fragment or the accuracy of a piece of testimony is accepted by the scholarly community, the information we thus possess is so piecemeal that serious problems arise in determining what the given Pre-Socratic *meant* when he said what we have agreed he did say. Once again, ample room exists for scholarly disagreement, which duly occurs. Lastly, when we notice that what has been preserved is the result of a selection procedure that was no doubt biased by the interests of those ancient authors who quoted and reported on the Pre-Socratics, many legitimate doubts are possible about the role and place of the preserved material in the larger body of thought from which it was selected.

The student must, then, keep in mind two facts about *all* discussions of the Pre-Socratics (including this discussion). First, our knowledge of what they said and meant is quite precarious. The situation is analogous to that of a paleontologist who has to infer the size, shape, and behavioral characteristics of some prehistoric animal from, say, a fossilized molar embedded in a fragment of a jawbone. Second, in consequence of that evidential situation, everyone attempting to learn about the Pre-Socratics must be prepared to accept that some expert or the other has disagreed with, or would disagree with, virtually *any* claim made about Pre-Socratic philosophy.

On the other hand, students should also be aware that there is extensive and drawn-out argumentation in Pre-Socratic studies about the acceptability of interpretations and such detailed examination is conducted in light of broadly shared standards. By now, general agreement has been secured in the Pre-Socratic scholarly community about many issues, both large and small. Differences of opinion about how to understand particular thinkers and texts face severe constraints on acceptability. Not anything goes.

BIBLIOGRAPHY

Students learning about the Pre-Socratics from this (or any other) text should be advised that additional reading would be very profitable. This short text considers all issues only partially and omits some matters entirely. Moreover, given the disagreements already mentioned, acquaintance with other views will deepen your understanding greatly.

To help the reader pursue further studies, I have made bibliographic recommendations of two types. In the following annotations, I have discussed several good surveys that can be useful to students who want to augment their knowledge of Pre-Socratic philosophy. Also, at the end of many chapters I have referred to works that are helpful about the subject of that particular chapter.

W. K. C. Guthrie, *History of Greek Philosophy*, 6 vols. (Cambridge, England: Cambridge University Press, 1962–1981). Volumes 1 and 2 cover the Pre-Socratics: both are available in paperback.

> *An extremely literate and readable survey. Guthrie's scholarly judgments are always sensible. The book is also thorough, attempting to discuss every issue and every scholarly dispute. That, and the consequent length of the book, can hinder the beginning student. Nonetheless, follow-up reading in Guthrie is highly recommended.*

G. S. Kirk, J. E. Raven, and M. Schofield, *The Pre-Socratic Philosophers*, 2nd ed. (Cambridge, England: Cambridge University Press, 1983). Paperback.

> *In contrast with Guthrie, this survey is compact. Because the authors attempt to offer their judgments on virtually all issues concerning the Pre-Socratics, the compactness of the discussion is a drawback. So is the extensive use of Greek in the body of the text (although translations always appear).*
>
> *However, with a little effort on the student's part, this book is helpful (and it also affords an opportunity to learn a little philosophical Greek).*

Richard D. McKirahan, Jr., *Philosophy Before Socrates: An Introduction with Texts and Commentary* (Indianapolis/Cambridge, England: Hackett Publishing, 1994).

> *The most recent general scholarly book on the Pre-Socratics that includes both translations of the texts and philosophical discussion of the ideas. Very useful.*

J. M. Robinson, *An Introduction to Early Greek Philosophy* (Boston: Houghton Mifflin, 1968). Paperback.

> *Unlike the preceding books, Robinson's book is not addressed to the scholar but rather seems aimed at something like an undergraduate audience. It is thus easier for the beginner. On the other hand, it is not of the same intellectual stature as the other works, lacking the crispness of view and insight that is helpful to an introductory reader.*

Jonathan Barnes, *The Pre-Socratic Philosophers*, 2 vols. (London: Routledge & Kegan Paul, 1979). Available in a one-volume paperback.

> *Barnes's book is a survey, but it is both less and more than that. His aim is to examine critically the arguments offered in support of the central theses of the various Pre-Socratics. Hence, the book is less descriptive and more a piece of philosophical criticism than the other surveys. It is also very witty and often challenges typical interpretations. Highly recommended for those who want to extend their study of the Pre-Socratics.*

Sir Karl Popper, "Back to the Pre-Socratics," reprinted in D. J. Furley and R. E. Allen, eds., *Studies in Pre-Socratic Philosophy*, Vol. I (New York: Humanities Press, 1970) and in K. Popper, *Conjectures and Refutations* (London: Routledge & Kegan Paul, 1963).

> *Popper's Aristotelian Society Presidential Address of 1958 is worth reading to see how a distinguished twentieth-century philosopher regards the relationship between the Pre-Socratics and present philosophy.*

H. Diels, *Die Fragmente der Vorsokratiker*, ed. W. Kranz, 5th ed. (Berlin: Weidmann, 1934).

> *One lost quasi-bibliographic reference can be made. The fragments of and testimony about the Pre-Socratics are scattered throughout many ancient works, so it was highly desirable that they be collected together in a single work. That was accomplished by a German scholar named Diels in a book entitled* Die Fragmente der Vorsokratiker. *(The fifth edition was edited by a man named Kranz, so that edition is referred to as Diels-Kranz.) An English translation of the fragments, somewhat out of date by now, was made by Kathleen Freeman, entitled* Ancilla to the Pre-Socratic Philosophers *(Cambridge, Mass.: Harvard University Press, 1957).*
>
> *Diels's book performs a function in addition to that of collecting all the fragments of Pre-Socratic philosophy in one place. He assigned each fragment an arbitrary number, so that there would be a simple and standard manner of referring to a given fragment. Hence, in this book, when I refer to Fragment 16 in speaking of, say, Heraclitus, that means the sixteenth fragment of Heraclitus as listed by Diels. Other works on the Pre-Socratics use Diels as a standard reference, though in referring to the sixteenth fragment of Heraclitus they may say D16 or DK 16 (for Diels or Diels-Kranz).*

HISTORICAL BACKGROUND

To study the origin and early growth of philosophy intelligently, we must know something about the cultural and historical setting for that intellectual development. In fact, social circumstances were more than a mere setting for the early stages of philosophy. When an intellectual discipline has not yet acquired a historical tradition and so has no (or few) internal and technical problems, the social environment significantly shapes and directs the first steps in creating the field of study. Such social influence was even greater than normal at the start of philosophy. What happened then was not simply the birth of a particular discipline, but the *origin of rational inquiry* itself.

HELLAS

The first thing to learn is that the Greeks were not Greek. There is more to that paradox than the fact that the word "Greek," which is of relatively recent origin, is the name applied to them by others. They came to call themselves Hellenes around the time when we pick up the story, namely in the late seventh century B.C.E.

They recognized themselves to be a single people by the possession of a common language, although several major dialects existed, and by shared pieces of culture. They did not, as modern peoples are inclined to do, tend to identify themselves with a particular piece of ground. (One could even say that no *place* was Greece, although that would be a slight exaggeration.) Every colony of Hellenes running their own lives was a piece of Hellas.

THE AEGEAN

What we today call the Greek mainland has always (in terms of human habitation) formed but one part of a larger geographical area whose center is the Aegean Sea. (Commencing now, a reader should follow this tale on the relevant maps.) That area includes the Greek mainland, the Aegean islands,

Crete, Cyprus, and the west coast of Asia Minor (which today is Turkey). Similarities of climate, terrain, and resources in the Aegean area have tended to create a similar way of life for the various peoples who have lived there.

Human habitation of the area goes back at least 40,000 years. Stone Age cultures evolved over the thousands of years. A significant change began soon after 3000 B.C.E. The techniques of metalworking that had been developed in the Near East began entering the Aegean area and spread quickly. The Aegean Bronze Age began about 2800 B.C.E., although it was some centuries thereafter (say 2500 B.C.E.) before the Aegean peoples became dependent on metal.

CRETE

The first great civilization to develop in the Aegean was on the island of Crete. A Neolithic culture acquired the new metal technology about 2500 B.C.E. and began to evolve. The high point of the culture was between 2000 and 1600 B.C.E. During those centuries, political power was extended over the area and the civilization grew correspondingly wealthy. A sophisticated artistic culture was created.

The Cretans also invented a system of writing, something that has helped enormously in learning about the civilization. First came a type of hieroglyphic script, followed by a more or less syllabic script now called Linear A.

From that evolved a further system we call Linear B. The language of Linear B was deciphered in a great breakthrough in 1952. The surprising result was that the language was an early form of Greek, the language of the mainland. Linear A has not been deciphered and is presumably the language of the native Cretan peoples.

The decoding of Linear B has led to the following interpretation of Cretan history. Sometime around 1600 to 1550 B.C.E. mainlanders speaking a version of Greek took control of the chief center of Cretan power, Knossos, and came to rule the rest of the island to an unknown extent. Around 1400 B.C.E. occurred a mysterious event that produced the total collapse of Cretan civilization. Many theories have been offered as to what happened, such as a massive earthquake, but no agreement exists. Crete simply was no longer the center of Aegean civilization. The Greek mainland became the locus of power in the region.

MYCENAEAN CIVILIZATION

Beginning about 2200 B.C.E., people speaking an early form of Greek had begun moving into the Greek mainland from somewhere north. Of course, communities had long been established there. Having been part of the periphery of Cretan civilization, those people were more civilized than the invaders. Although the archaeological record shows a significant amount of destruction in the period 2000–1700 B.C.E., in the long run the new arrivals intermingled, sexually and culturally, with those already inhabiting the area. The outcome was a new civilization, combining elements drawn from both native culture and that of the Greeks, as well as important Cretan influences.

That new civilization did not arise overnight, however. Archaeological findings show very little by way of material development for the first 600 years. About 1600 B.C.E. the way of life of those peoples inhabiting the mainland suddenly improved. Why that spurt came about is unknown. A place called Mycenae (*My-seen'-ee*) led the way in that cultural development:

> Mycenae suddenly became a center of wealth and power, and of a warrior civilization, without an equal in this region. Soon other important centers rose in central and southern Greece, and influences then radiated to the Aegean islands, and the coasts of Asia Minor and Syria in the east, and to Sicily and southern Italy in the west. (Finley, 1970, p. 47)

It seems clear that men from this new Greek-speaking civilization came to control Knossos and thus Cretan civilization shortly after 1600 B.C.E., leaving Linear B as the record of their conquest. When civilized life on Crete collapsed around 1400 B.C.E., the Mycenaean civilization became the only power in the area, a fact marked by the building of many palace-fortresses at various centers on the mainland about that time.

Mycenaean power was dispersed among a large number of separate domains, all rather small, each ruled by a king who was the chief among an elite of warrior aristocrats (no doubt descendants of the Greek invaders). Both the physical remains and the Greek legends show that the chief activity of that ruling class was fighting. The best known of those constant military actions was the Trojan War, the lengthy invasion and ultimate destruction of the kingdom of Troy, situated on the coast of Asia Minor, about 1200 B.C.E. by the Mycenaean principalities.

THE COLLAPSE OF MYCENAEAN CIVILIZATION AND THE DARK AGE

Between about 1200 and 1000 B.C.E. the Bronze Age civilization of Mycenae collapsed, and there was a large migration of Greeks from the mainland to the Aegean islands and to the coast of Asia Minor. The Greeks themselves later attributed that movement of population to an invasion by other Greek-speaking peoples from the north (the so-called Dorian invasion). Contemporary archaeologists, while finding both a destruction of most Mycenaean sites during that period and a simultaneous extensive depopulation of the area, cannot, however, identify any signs of a major invasion. Thus what caused the end of the Bronze Age on the mainland and the associated flight of people to the islands and Asia Minor is a current archaeological and historical mystery.

The period 1200 to 800 B.C.E. is known as the (Greek) Dark Age. The mainland population was much smaller than previously, and much poorer. There were no large buildings, and technology and artistry were at a low ebb.

Yet during those centuries, when the conditions of life were so low, another new civilization was being created: what was to become classical Greece. The remnants of Mycenaean civilization, who had fled to the coast of Asia Minor (known as Ionia) and to the islands, led that building of a new Greek civilization. Some centuries elapsed before the mainland caught up.

THE *ILIAD* AND THE *ODYSSEY*

Around 800 B.C.E. the Ionian Greeks reacquired the means of a written language (the loss of Linear B had been one consequence of the collapse of Mycenaean civilization). This time the Phoenician alphabet was borrowed and modified to create a Greek written language. The ability to write and read spread rather rapidly.

About 750 B.C.E. were written the two great Greek poems, two of the world's great pieces of literature: the *Iliad* and the *Odyssey*. They were, and are, attributed to a man named Homer but were probably written by two different men. It would be more accurate to say that the poems were *written down* at that time, for they are the outcome of centuries of oral poetry produced by the professional bards who traveled throughout the Greek world during the Dark Age.

The poems are about events in the Mycenaean world—the poets were singing of a lost heroic world very different from their own. But the poems actually reveal much more of the life of the Dark Age than they do of Mycenaean civilization.

> In sum the Homeric poems retain a certain measure of Mycenaean "things"—places, arms, weapons, chariots—but little of Mycenaean institutions or culture. The break had been too sharp. As the pre-1200 civilization receded into the past, the bards could not avoid "modernizing" the behavior and the social background of their heroes. . . . [The] picture . . . is in general one of the Dark Age; and on the whole of the earlier half of that age. . . .
>
> The world of Agamemnon and Achilles and Odysseus [as represented in the poems] was one of petty kings and nobles, who possessed the best land and considerable flocks, and lived a seignorial existence, in which local wars and raids flourished. The noble household was the center of activity and power. How much power depended on wealth, personal prowess, connections by marriage and alliance. . . . The king

with power was judge, law-giver and commander, and there were accepted ceremonies, rituals and conventions and a code of honor by which nobles lived . . . , but there was no bureaucratic apparatus, no formalized legal system or constitutional machinery. . . . Tension between king and nobles was chronic, struggles for power frequent. (Finley, 1970, pp. 84–85)

ARCHAIC GREECE

The dominant culture from 800 to 500 B.C.E. is usually called archaic Greece, and the period is part of the historical era, because written records became possible with the development of a written language. Writing and the spread of literacy were not the only signs that a sophisticated new civilization was emerging. The *Iliad* and the *Odyssey* were put into their final (written) form then. They became the source of a strong and increasingly complex poetic tradition. During that same period, philosophy and also science had their origin and initial growth. Also, in archaic Greece the visual arts underwent one of the most significant changes they have ever experienced.

Although it is impossible here to detail the enormous changes that occurred in the life of the Greeks during those centuries, one development cannot be omitted: that of the Greek *polis*. The word *polis* (from which derives our word "politics" and its relatives) is usually translated "city-state," but (as every translator points out) that is misleading. The Greeks lived in small but independent communities. Such a community would consist of an urban center, which was often only a village, surrounded by the necessary agricultural land. Each of those communities was, at least in aspiration, politically independent. That is, each was, in modern terminology, a separate state. During the Dark Age, those small states were ruled by petty kings, as described in the quote from Finley (1970). About 800 B.C.E., however, the institution of kingship began to vanish, leaving power (initially at least) in the hands of the landowning aristocracy. Those nonmonarchical, self-governing communities became the Greek *polei*, the central and characteristic institution of ancient Greece.

Those city-states were small, both in size and in population. Athens was a giant. It comprised about 1,000 square miles (modern Rhode Island is 20 percent larger) and had, at about 430 B.C.E., a total population of around 250,000. However, only one other *polis* was close to Athens in population, fewer than ten had more than 50,000 inhabitants, while the vast majority had 5,000 or fewer people living within their borders. And *many* city-states made up ancient Greece: several hundreds.

Some of that political fragmentation was due to the geography of the area. Much of the inhabitable land consisted of small valleys, peninsulas, and islands. But there is more to the story than that: the Greeks came to believe that the *polis* was the only proper structure for a civilized life. The peoples of the east (Persia, Egypt) were barbarians—they did not speak Greek, and they lived without freedom in vast empires, under a central authority.

Along with the rise of the *polis*, a second major phenomenon of the archaic period was a great expansion of the Greek-speaking people. About 750 B.C.E. began two centuries of so-called colonizing. By 500 B.C.E. the Greeks had settled on the "northern, western and southern shores of the Black Sea, through western Asia Minor and Greece proper (with the Aegean islands) to much of Sicily and southern Italy, then continuing west along both shores of the Mediterranean to Cyrene in Libya and to Marseilles and some Spanish coastal sites. Wherever they went they settled on the edge of the sea, not in the hinterland" (Finley, 1970, p. 93). In each place, they established a new *polis*—not really a colony of the founding city, but another free and independent community, perhaps with ties of friendship to the mother *polis*.

What caused that exodus? One cause was a population explosion, produced no doubt by increasing prosperity. But the increased number of people aggravated a developing social crisis in the existing city-states. With the growing prosperity following the Dark Age, a middle class had come into being. These new people became as wealthy as members of the reigning elite, the large landowners descended from the old warrior aristocracy, and they demanded a share of political power. In sharp contrast was the large mass of working farmers, becoming more and more in debt to the landowners and so more subject to their demands. Both groups raised up a plea for justice, for some measure of political power in the *polis*. One way by which a *polis* might temporarily alleviate those internal strains was to send excess population off to found a new community.

One central theme in the history of the archaic period is the story of how different city-states dealt with the problems of prosperity, population growth, and political unrest. Other than the colonization solution, two other main developments must be noted. The *polis* of Sparta solved the problems by creating a military way of life for its aristocracy and by reducing the rest of its population to agricultural serfs. Athens went in the opposite direction, making itself into an urban *polis*, opening up power to more and more of its citizens until it became a democracy. These two were the major city-states in Greece, and their values and institutions were evolving in contrary directions. Thus the seeds of future troubles between them were sown.

THE ORIGINS OF CLASSICAL GREECE

In the sixth century B.C.E., the Persian empire began expanding, its westward push extending its power (through what is now Turkey) to the Aegean about 550 B.C.E. The numerous Greek city-states of Ionia (the eastern shore of the Aegean) were subjected to Persian rule. In 499 B.C.E. the Ionian states revolted and asked the communities of the mainland for assistance. Little aid was dispatched, although Athens did send about twenty ships, and the revolt was put down.

The Persians seem to have concluded that they could not continue to hold Ionia without doing something about the Greeks across the Aegean. In 490 B.C.E. the Persian king, Darius, sent an expeditionary force against the mainland. Although Sparta had the only strong army on the Greek side, Sparta never got around to fighting. The Athenians, almost alone, decisively defeated the Persians at Marathon.

Anticipating that the Persians would make another attempt, the Athenians used the proceeds from a recently discovered silver mine to construct a new fleet. In 480 B.C.E. the Persians came again, this time in a full-scale invasion. The Athenians withdrew from Athens, boarded their fleet, and allowed Athens to be burned. But they then trapped the Persian fleet and destroyed it at Salamis. The Persian army, cut off by the loss of its transport, tried to get out but was destroyed in the course of several battles, the Greek army fighting under Spartan leadership.

What followed the Persian Wars (as the victors called them) has been described as an intoxication of the Greeks. They had twice within ten years smashed the attempts of a great empire to conquer them and their city-states. They reached the conclusion that their way of life was obviously superior to any other. Since the Athenians had led the way in these events, they drew the conclusion more explicitly than others. The outpouring of power and talent produced by the success in the Persian Wars constituted what is called classical Greece.

THE ATHENIAN EMPIRE AND
THE PELOPONNESIAN WAR

Athens and her fleet now controlled the Aegean, completely clearing it of Persian power in the next ten years. To assist in that enterprise, Athens set up a league, under her leadership, of the numerous Aegean island city-states. But when the danger was past and the fleet in control of the Aegean, Athens insisted that the league continue. Coercion was necessary to keep many of the states in the alliance. Athens now had an empire. The member states stopped contributing men and ships and instead sent money. Not long after, the treasury was moved to Athens.

With the new riches, Athens rebuilt herself, making her the physical center of Greek civilization. With political power and the accumulated wealth of the league, Athens also became the intellectual and artistic center of the culture.

That expansion of power and prestige had its dangers—it brought Athens into greater conflict with Sparta, hitherto the major power. The conflict became unresolvable, with war finally breaking out in 431 B.C.E. Before it ended in 404 B.C.E., the Peloponnesian War had sucked in most of the Greek *polei* on one side or the other. (The war is the subject of the first great piece of historical writing, Thucydides' *[Thu-sid'-ee-deez] History of the Peloponnesian War.* Thucydides, an Athenian, wrote it before the end of the conflict.) Athens was finally worn down and defeated. Despite the misery of such a protracted conflict, the period was the Golden Age of Greece, a time when Greece and especially Athens formed one of the most brilliant of human civilizations.

THE END OF CLASSICAL GREECE

Although it was not obvious then, the defeat of Athens and her loss of the empire after the Peloponnesian War led to the downfall of classical Greece. What was lost when Athens was stripped of her client states was the only possible means of unifying the many highly independent Greek city-states, at least of unifying them under Greek control. A power vacuum had been created in the Aegean.

At the end of the war, Sparta installed in Athens a group of rulers. These Thirty Tyrants, as they were called, lasted in power only a year. A revolt in 403 B.C.E. restored the Athenian democracy. Between then and 338 B.C.E., Greece was in constant turmoil. In 359 B.C.E., Phillip II became king of Macedonia, a country northwest of Greece whose people were ethnically and linguistically related to the Greeks. Phillip began accumulating influence in Greece, although Athens attempted to resist. The Greeks were defeated at the battle of Chaeronea in 338 B.C.E., and Phillip's victory there made him, in effect, the overlord of Greece. The Greeks struggled against that domination, but resistance was ended for good in 335 B.C.E. when Phillip's son, Alexander, came to the throne and put down all opposition. Alexander (the Great) then set out to conquer the world, largely succeeding in his aim by the time of his death in 323 B.C.E.

Classical Greece was then at an end. The Greeks were now part of a gigantic empire with no self-rule. Greek culture lived on—Alexander spread it all over the Middle East—but the *polis* was no longer the ruling institution of the Greeks' own lives, and that was what had been at the root of classical Greece.

BIBLIOGRAPHY

M. I. Finley, *The Ancient Greeks* (London: Chatto and Windus, 1963).
   An extremely good survey of the events just discussed. Very readable.
H. D. F. Kitto, *The Greeks,* rev. ed. (Harmondsworth, England: Penguin, 1957).
   Covers the same ground as Finley, but in a different spirit. Again, quite readable.
Frank Frost, *Greek Society,* 2nd ed. (Lexington, Mass.: Heath, 1980).
   A useful book about ancient Greek society.
M. I. Finley, *Early Greece* (New York: Norton, 1970).
   More specialized than the preceding books.

HESIOD AND THE GREEK COSMOGONICAL MYTHS

It is necessary to begin this chapter with some terminology. The word *cosmology* refers to the investigation of the structure and order of the universe as a whole. The word *cosmogony* refers to the study of the history of the world order—of how the universe came to be the way that it is. Both words are derived from the Greek *kosmos*, a word that originally meant "order" of any sort, passed on to refer to that particular order that can be seen in the heavens, and ultimately came to mean "universe."

Although the two words cover two distinguishable provinces of inquiry, in the modern world the word *cosmogony* is not much used. Scientists and philosophers talk mostly of cosmology and consider as a special part of cosmological studies the investigation of the origins (and also the future) of the present world order. In what follows, I often adopt the modern terminology and speak of cosmology as including both studies.

Note one further point. A cosmogony—an account of how things came to be the way that they are—presupposes a cosmology. One must have some idea, at least, of how things *are* in order to talk of how they *came to be* that way.

Anthropologists tell us that all primitive peoples (and undoubtedly all peoples generally) have some account of how the universe is structured and of how it came to be that way. Today we call those primitive accounts *myths* and, for reasons to be mentioned later, we distinguish them from *science*, which is our way of accounting for the origin and order of the world. Thus, we can say that primitive peoples have mythological cosmogonies and cosmologies. To understand the beginnings of Western philosophy, we must start with the cosmogonical myths of the Greeks.

HESIOD

The Greeks rated Hesiod *(Hee'-see-odd)* second only to Homer as a poet. Hesiod, who lived sometime between 750 and 700 B.C.E., was a farmer who also wrote poetry. His *Works and Days*, about day-to-day life on a small farm, gives us a picture of Greek life quite different from the world of the heroes. For our purposes, however, his main work is the *Theogony*.

The ancient Greeks, like other primitive peoples, had their accounts of the arrangement and ancestry of the world. But instead of one tale, there had come to be, for historical and geographical reasons, several stories varying in this and that feature. The *Theogony* was Hesiod's attempt to bring some order into those myths. He took the existing tales and tried to set out a consistent account, adding some items and ideas himself.

The word *theogony* means "creation of the gods." Hesiod's main aim in the work is to discuss the origins and history of the gods who were, of course, a very prominent feature of the universe. However, in talking about the gods and in attempting to produce a unified account, he cannot help but say something about the creation of the universe and about its structure.

THE GREEK COSMOLOGY

Hesiod's interest was in the Greek creation stories. Hence the cosmological items, the representation of the present structure of the universe, appear only incidentally and by implication. That is because he undoubtedly relied on the standard Greek picture of the organization of the world.

In that scheme, the earth seems to be a sort of column, the inhabited earth being the flat upper end; the other end, Tartarus, is far off and very obscure. Over the earth arches Heaven, and the top end of the column is encircled by a stream called Ocean. This universe was certainly thought by the Greeks to be quite limited in size.

HESIOD'S CREATION MYTH

Hesiod presents a story of how the present arrangement of the universe came to be. For him, there was a time when the present order of things did not exist. What was the original condition of the world, before it began evolving into the world as we know it? For Hesiod, in the beginning there was a *primordial unity*—the universe was originally an undifferentiated blob.

The first stage of development was the production of a *gap* between what came to be Heaven and Earth, a separation into two parts of the original unity. Note that the word *chaos* in Greek originally meant "gap"; that is what it means in the part of the poem given here. Hesiod tells how our organized world began:

> Tell me all this, you Muses who have your homes on Olympos, from the beginning, and tell who was first to come forth among them. First of all there came Chaos, and after him came Gaia [Earth] of the broad breast, to be the unshakable foundation of all the immortals who keep

the crests of snowy Olympos, and Tartarus the foggy, [born] in the pit
of the wide-wayed earth, and Eros, who is Love, handsomest among all
the immortals, who breaks the limb's strength, who in all gods, in all
human beings, overpowers the intelligence in the breast, and all their
shrewd planning.

From Chaos was born Erebos, the dark, and black Night, and from
Night again Aither and Hemera, the day, were begotten, for she lay in
love with Erebos and conceived and bore these two.

But Gaia's first born was one who matched her every dimension,
Ouranos [Heaven], the starry sky, to cover her all over. . . . Without
any sweet act of love she produced the barren sea, Pontos, seething
in his fury of waves, and after this she lay with Ouranos, and bore him
Okeanos the ocean-stream. . . . After these her youngest-born was
devious-devising Kronos, most terrible of her children; and he hated
his strong father. (*Theogony*, ll. 114–138, trans. Richard Lattimore, in
Hesiod [Ann Arbor: University of Michigan Press, 1959])

Two things should be observed about the story in those lines: the items
composing the universe are personalized and the details of creation are
thought of in sexual terms.

What explanation for that initial separation of the two main parts of the
universe did Hesiod offer? In these lines, Earth produces new cosmic features chiefly through sexual contact with Heaven, who lies over and on top
of her. Hesiod goes on to say that Heaven refused to allow these new beings
to be born; Ouranos kept them pushed down within Earth.

Earth, being both in pain and angry at Ouranos for his treatment of
their offspring, plotted with their youngest, Kronos. Kronos went forth with
a sickle, and when Heaven "came on bringing night with him, and desiring
love he embraced Gaia and lay over her stretched out complete," Kronos cas-
trated his father. Presumably Ouranos drew back in pain—and *thus* was the
gap between heaven and earth created.

Hesiod tried to systematize the tales—he obviously did not wholly succeed. Others who came after him attempted to improve on his account and
tried to systematize in the same kind of way, using the *same kinds of concepts
and explanations*. That is, for Hesiod and those who followed his manner, the
constituents of the universe were *personal beings* (divine in fact) and the
causes of the universe's development were *personal causes*—sexuality, hatred,
jealousy, and so forth.

Other thinkers, however, were also interested in the universe and its history, and made a break with that way of thinking, with those ideas and with
that outlook we call mythological. We are now in a position to examine those
people—the philosophers.

BIBLIOGRAPHY

Henri and H. A. Frankfort, John A. Wilson, Thurkild Jacobsen, and William A. Irwin, *The Intellectual Adventures of Ancient Man* (Chicago: University of Chicago Press, 1946).

> *About cosmological thought in the ancient Near East. See especially the final chapter for the transition from mythological thought to philosophy in Greece.*

MILETUS AND THE
BEGINNING OF PHILOSOPHY

The first thinkers who are counted as philosophers were from Miletus *(My-leet'-us)*, the chief *polis* of Ionian Greece, a thriving seaport and commercial center. Because of their place of origin, these three thinkers—Thales (about 624–545 B.C.E.), Anaximander (about 610–545 B.C.E.), and Anaximenes (about 580–500 B.C.E.)—are usually called the *Milesians*.

THE CULTURAL BACKGROUND

To understand something of why Ionia was the place of origin of the earliest philosophical activity, it is necessary to recall a little Ionian history. About 1200 B.C.E., migrations began from the mainland to the Aegean islands and to the far coast of Asia Minor. For whatever reason, a cultural revival began among the migrants in Ionia and then spread to their place of origin. The Phoenician alphabet was adapted there, and so a written language developed again. Homer, an Ionian Greek, left behind a poetic tradition that continued over the next two centuries. During that same period, say 750 to 550 B.C.E., Ionian Greece became a quite sophisticated new civilization. Commerce flourished, wealth and well-being increased rapidly. The upper classes, from whom the poets and philosophers came, acquired leisure time, a prerequisite for intellectual activity. Furthermore, because of its geographical location at an intersection of various cultures, and because of its commercial connections, other ways of thinking and living began impressing themselves on the Ionian Greeks, especially in its leading *polis,* Miletus.

Nonmythological cosmology developed as part of a much broader intellectual movement occurring simultaneously in Ionia. At the time, the Greek word *historie* meant "inquiry" or "research" (before becoming fixed as the name of that particular field of study we call "history"). Interest in inquiring into the history and constitution of the universe was only one strand, although a central one in the growth of Ionian *historie.* Astronomy and arithmetic were imported from Babylonia and geometry from Egypt, but were

17

quickly transformed into Greek specialties. That outburst of curiosity laid the (Greek) foundations of other technical studies, such as engineering and rational medicine. What might be called cultural anthropology—travels to visit other peoples and reporting on their customs, including their scientific activities—and geography, which grew out of those travels, were important and (popular) elements of that new interest in learning about the world surrounding them. In short, the birth of philosophy was anything but an isolated intellectual phenomenon.

THE MILESIANS AND RATIONAL EXPLANATIONS

The Milesians initiated, though they certainly did not complete, a revolution in the way to think about the world and its history. Like any revolution, this one involved two sorts of activity: overturning the existing structures and then replacing them with something new.

In this case, mythological explanations were to be overthrown. In accounting for the course of world history and for its present behavior, there were no longer to be (continual) references to humanlike beings and to humanlike motives. That kind of notion was to be (largely) expunged from descriptions and accounts of the proceedings of the natural world.

We have no reason to believe that the program was aimed at *wholly* eliminating references to gods and motives from the study of the cosmos. For the Milesians and for their scientific successors down through the centuries, it has been an open question, and very often a bone of contention, as to how far rationality demands that scientific explanations be free of religious concepts. Certainly those who first began putting forward the new model of rational explanations of nature did not conceive of their project as requiring *total* elimination of religious references.

The other side of the revolutionary program was to produce some new set of ideas that would enable nonmythical understanding of the workings of the world. Here, too, the Milesians had some success. Theirs was the first attempt to *reduce* the multiplicity of objects of nature and the variety of changes in the natural world to a *simple, orderly* basis. Their attempt to explain the diversity of nature and its processes in a simple, uniform way is part of the scientific enterprise to this day.

THALES

Even given the general inadequacy of our information about the Pre-Socratics, Thales (*Thay'-leez*) constitutes a special problem. We know very little about his cosmological thought, and there may have been little to know in the first place. In fact, even Aristotle, who was the first historian of philosophy and who is virtually the sole source of our information about Thales, knew little about his cosmological ideas.

Because of the great lack of information about his cosmology and the uncertainty of what we have, scholars have disagreed about his importance. Ought we to say that Thales was the first philosopher, as Aristotle calls him, or ought we to think of him as a predecessor of the real philosophical-cosmological work? The tradition derived from Aristotle has placed him first in the historical sequence, and although some modern scholars would disagree, this book also places him first.

Thales' lifetime ran, approximately, from 624 to 545 B.C.E. It is clear that he was a man of practical wisdom and experience. The Greeks honored their wise men of the early sixth century B.C.E. by constructing lists of the Seven Sages. Although those lists varied from one time and place to another, Thales seems to have been unanimously selected for inclusion and was often put at the top of the list. His reputation was based on achievements in a variety of fields: politics, engineering, astronomy, and mathematics. He was credited with introducing geometry into Greece. Most probably, he learned empirical geometry in Egypt and impressed his fellow Greeks with his ability to use it in measurement, though leaving it to later Greek mathematicians to develop the theory of geometry. He predicted a solar eclipse in 585 B.C.E.—which duly occurred. That prediction and other astronomical interests indicate that he had learned the advanced computational astronomy of Babylonia.

Thales' Cosmology

Aristotle reports that Thales believed the earth rests on water. That was not a native Greek notion; and in Hesiod, water encircles the earth and is not said to be under it. Yet throughout the Near East, Egyptian, Babylonian, and Hebraic mythological cosmologies commonly claimed that the earth rested on water. See *Psalms:* Yahweh "stretched out the earth upon the waters" (Ps.136:6), he "founded it upon the seas, and established it upon the floods" (Ps. 24:2). So very probably Thales imported a new cosmological idea into Greek thought from his contacts with Near Eastern cultures.

Also, evidence exists that Thales employed the idea that the earth rests on water to answer two other, more specialized, questions. According to Aristotle, Thales held that the earth stays in place through floating like a log. That is, Thales offered this as an *explanation* of how the earth is supported in space. Thales may also have used the idea that the earth floats on water to explain earthquakes: they are due to the movement of the water that supports the earth. Notice that both these explanations are in terms of *natural* substances and *natural* processes. No mention is made of some humanlike being holding the world on his or her shoulders or striking the ground in a fit of anger. That is, Thales' explanations were not mythological.

Thales' Cosmogony

Those Near Eastern mythologies also told that in the beginning the universe was nothing but an expanse of water, a watery chaos. From the fact that

Thales drew on those myths and from a comment of Aristotle's, it is fairly certain that Thales also held such a view: that at one time the universe consisted of nothing but water and out of that primordial water developed our present differentiated universe.

Here it is appropriate to indicate one of the reasons why it is permissible to call Thales the first philosopher. In Hesiod, the entities forming the universe were thought of as quasi-personal beings, Heaven and Earth, and the act that formed a differentiated universe was the work of such a personal being acting from human motives. So too in the Near Eastern stories, humanlike beings acting in humanlike ways are held to be responsible for constructing a developed universe. Thales did not think that way—the original water was not personified, and there is no reason to believe that he thought of the original act of creation as a humanlike deed. Just as in explaining the support of the earth and the cause of earthquakes, Thales was talking in *naturalistic* terms. A significant part of the justification for calling him the first philosopher lies in the fact that he abandoned (or was working at abandoning) mythological formulations of explanatory concepts.

The Stuff of the World

There is a second source of the claim that Thales was a philosopher as opposed to a mythmaker. Someone who says that the world long ago came from water might think that the present world had water as an *ancestor.* That would be a genealogical history of the universe, just as we find in Hesiod. Yet Aristotle's account shows that Thales probably had quite a different idea: long ago the world came from water—and *everything (still) is water.* That primordial water has not disappeared, as an ancestor would have. Rather, it has been transformed and now appears in a variety of disguises as all the objects of the universe. In such a view, "water is the continuing, hidden constituent of all things. . . . [W]ater, as well as being the cosmogonical source, is also involved in the very essence of the developed world" (Kirk, Raven, and Schofield, 1983, p. 94).

That cosmological idea was wholly new. Thales was talking, as no one had previously done, of the *stuff of which the world is made.* In short, Thales raised the issue of what we today call *matter theory.*

Why water as the stuff? On this topic even Aristotle had to guess. The most likely conjecture as to what led him to declare that all things are water is the following: Thales started from the idea that the universe had its origin as a watery chaos—the Near Eastern cosmogonical belief that he had adopted. He then realized that the development of other objects from that water could be a *transformation,* rather than a replacement, of the original stuff. The water would remain in a variety of new forms.

That such a thing was possible for water *could* be supported by empirical observation (although the idea that Thales did so is pure conjecture, a conjecture begun by Aristotle). Water can be *seen* to be transformed into other states. By evaporation, water turns into steam and hence apparently into air. Water freezes and becomes a solid. Both processes can be reversed—rain and condensation seem to be a return of water from air and melting turns a solid into water. These facts could be used to hold that the things were water all along.

The idea of such transformations, with the original substances remaining in a disguise, was also strongly suggested by the Greek myths. Gods and goddesses frequently appeared to human beings in a variety of forms— Proteus, in particular, had the power to appear as an enormous number of things. Mythology and observation could have cooperated to lead Thales to the creative step of thinking that all objects coming after the original water were nothing else but that water in various disguises.

Living Matter

Primitive peoples tend to be animistic—to see features of the world that we now consider inanimate as alive or as inhabited by living beings, spirits. The Greeks, well down into historical times, certainly believed in such things, finding *daimons* and spirits of various kinds in many (as we today would say) natural objects.

Aristotle says that Thales thought that all things are full of gods. Such a view would undoubtedly be, in part, no more than an expression of the common animistic background of Greek belief. But it may have been more. For it is also reported that Thales, noticing that lodestone and amber (both of which have magnetic properties) have the power to move iron, concluded that these apparently inanimate objects are really alive, that they possessed *psyché*. In drawing such an inference, Thales may have been trying to extend the realm of the animate to objects that even his animistic contemporaries thought of as nonliving. And that *might* mean that Thales saw some connection between saying that all things are full of gods and saying that everything is water. Water to Thales might have been a divinity, an immortal being, something living that, precisely because it is living, is capable of self-initiated movement and change. Such a belief in living matter would explain what otherwise seems to be a serious omission in Thales' (and his successors') descriptions of the universe. There is no mention in the Milesians' account of the world of any agency that exists independently of the basic stuff and that would function to cause the various transformations and changes they were concerned to describe and to explain. But if the basic stuff is alive, then it is capable of producing such changes itself and there is no need to think that some other force exists to cause change.

ANAXIMANDER

Anaximander *(Ann-ax'-ee-mander)* is described in ancient sources as a younger contemporary and fellow townsman of Thales—that is, he was a

Milesian and lived about 610–545 B.C.E. Presumably there was an intellectual connection between the two, although it may not be legitimate to call Anaximander the pupil of Thales, as has been done. He was not made into a culture hero like Thales, so we know little of his life. He probably introduced the *gnomon,* a sundial, into Greece from Babylonia. More important, he was the first Greek to draw a map of the entire earth. Even more important, he, unlike Thales, wrote a book, a treatise, not a poem. This Ionian creation of the prose treatise was itself a part of demythologizing the world.

It would be impossible to write a book about Thales—there is not enough to be said. But there is enough to be said about Anaximander, and we do have a book about him (see Bibliography at the end of this chapter). Although we possess only a single fragment containing his actual words, a fair amount of testimony has survived concerning his thought, although the accuracy of some of it is in question. Many scholars have declared him to have the legitimate claim to being "the first philosopher," on two grounds: (1) we have more evidence (testimony) than in the case of Thales to support the claim, and (2) what he attempted to do was vastly more comprehensive than anything we can attribute to Thales. Whether or not we call him "first" in the tradition, it is certain that the power and breadth of his thought largely shaped the aims and outlines of subsequent philosophical and scientific developments.

The Cosmic Masses

Anaximander probably started with a description of the general structure and composition of the universe. Although some details are unclear, he conceived of the universe as consisting of at least four and probably five concentric areas of different stuffs. At the very center of everything is an area of earth; surrounding that is a layer of water; next is a vast expanse of air; and the final "observable" section is a realm of fire. (The fifth and outermost layer will be discussed later.)

That general scheme of the universe became the framework for future Greek cosmologies. Later thinkers only clarified it and introduced modifications in both detail and emphasis.

Anaximander did not wholly invent it. "The oldest Greek literary texts [Homer and Hesiod] recognize a simple division of the world into four parts or portions: earth, sea, heaven and the nether darkness occupied by Hades and Night" (Kahn, 1960, p. 152). Anaximander improved on the poetic scheme by clarifying the structural relations of these parts and by developing the notions of the atmosphere and the heavenly fire. Moreover, he greatly extended Thales' first step in demythologizing the universe: in the very act of treating more features of the universe than Thales had, he thus had more opportunity to do without mythological notions. He did not speak of Gaia (earth), Pontos (sea), and Ouranos (heaven). Those personal beings he naturalized as earth, water, and so on. Along with Thales, he was inventing a notion of nature—*physis,* in Greek. Only after the groundwork was laid could there be a distinction between the natural and the supernatural.

The Opposites

So far I have described Anaximander as having held that the universe is a structure composed of at least four kinds of stuff: earth, water, air, and fire. That description is inaccurate in an important respect. Actually, he thought the universe to be composed of *pairs of opposites,* especially of the hot and the cold, the wet and the dry. He made something like the following associations: the dry = earth, the wet = water, the cold = air, the hot = fire. Fire, for example, would be the visible embodiment of the *cosmological constituent* the hot.

As with the cosmic masses, what Anaximander introduced as a basic principle—the conception of the universe as consisting of pairs of opposites and especially the opposites cited here—became a central theme in subsequent Greek cosmological thought (as well as in Greek medical theory).

Change

Anaximander's view has been presented as if the universe were static, as if no changes occurred within that structural framework. But that picture of his view is wholly misleading. The universe, as he viewed it, is chiefly characterized by *ceaseless* alterations in the relationships of its constituents. Water is evaporated, drawn up into the air by heat, leaving the earth dry; the water returns as rain, along with bolts of heavenly fire and disturbances of the air, sometimes in such quantities as to flood the parched earth. The seasons change from wet to dry and back again. Each day starts out cool, grows hot, and cools again; these daily temperature cycles are analogous to seasonal cycles of hot and cold.

Anaximander, then, was *particularly* concerned with change, and especially with such changes. He saw his cosmological constituents interacting in cyclical, periodic patterns.

The Fragment

The one piece of Anaximander's writing still in existence is concerned with just those matters of change. This fragment can be translated as "Existing things perish into those things out of which they have come to be, as must be; for they pay reparation to each other for their injustice according to the ordinance of time."

The interpretation of this fragment has been much disputed by scholars. Nevertheless, we must give some account of what Anaximander meant by saying that.

The fragment is about "existing things." Let us take the phrase "existing things" to refer to the cosmological constituents. Anaximander's claim, then, is that an existing thing comes into being *out of* another existing thing *into* which it will inevitably perish. For example, the emergence of the rainy season out of the preceding dry season is conceived of as a generation of the wet out of the dry; later the wet (season) will generate the succeeding dry, and this will proceed to destroy the wet; and so on.

This process does not mean that one opposite of a pair *originally* came from the other. As we shall see, the opposites originated in something different. Rather, it must mean that in a world that already contains those existing things, the local advance of one means the local disappearance of its opposite. When the wet (season) comes to Greece, it does not follow that the wet has triumphed everywhere in the cosmos.

Some writers say that Anaximander held that the wet turns into the dry; that is, he took these changes as a process of one constituent being transformed into another, just as Thales seems to have thought water transformed into other things. It is not certain that is how he conceived of it. He might have thought of it genealogically so that the wet is an *offspring* of the dry and later in the cycle itself gives birth to the dry, which then destroys it.

The second crucial part of the fragment is the phrase "they [existing things] pay reparation to each other for their injustice." Anaximander conceives of the constantly changing relationships of the cosmic masses as perpetual *cosmic strife* among them.

This conception of the universe as a battleground for the elements lasted a very long time in Western thought. In the sixteenth century, Edmund Spenser wrote,

> The earth the air the water and the fire
> Then gan to range themselves in huge array,
> and with contrary forces to conspire
> Each against other by all means they may.

And in the seventeenth century, John Milton said,

> Hot, cold, wet and dry, four champions fierce
> Strive here for maistery.

That the hot, for example, destroys the cold is for Anaximander *wrongdoing, injustice*. The reason is that each of the cosmic constituents has its proper domain, and the intrusion of another constituent is thus an offense. In Homer and Hesiod, Zeus, Poseidon, and Hades are all allotted portions of the world to rule—the sky, the sea, and darkness, respectively, with the earth common to all. Any encroachment by one of those gods on the sphere of another is unjust and is to be resisted. Anaximander retains that scheme, although deposing the anthropomorphic gods in favor of natural entities.

The guilty will, however, pay for their injustice. The hot will give birth to the cold and will then pay for its previous injustice by being destroyed. But that destruction is also a piece of injustice, and so the cycle goes on.

What is most important about the fragment is the idea that those cosmic changes happen of *necessity*, that they come about (in Anaximander's words) "as must be." It does not rain because Zeus, for some reason or the other, decides it shall rain; rather, rain comes because, given certain antecedent conditions, it *must* rain. Natural changes do not happen as the result of whim on the part of divine beings—nor do they occur randomly. They occur in a *lawful* manner, "according to the ordinance of time"; that is, they happen when they are bound to happen.

Here in this idea of things happening lawfully, happening because such-and-such conditions exist, is the first recorded expression of a *conception of nature*, which is by now deeply embedded in Western culture, a conception that forms the basis of our rational and scientific culture.

Not surprisingly, in trying to work out that view Anaximander thought of nature in moral terms, thought of those changes as involving a *moral* necessity. He was familiar with the idea of religious, political, and moral law, and it was entirely understandable that he should formulate the first conception of *laws of nature* in those more familiar social terms. Nonetheless, this retention of anthropomorphism is very sophisticated: the personal gods are gone but the cosmic constituents are related in ways appropriate to human beings; namely, they stand in moral relations.

What the Cosmogonical Source of the Universe Was Not—and Why

Thales held that originally there was only water. In Anaximander's universe of earth, water, air, and fire, which was the stuff from which all the others began? The answer is "None of those."*

Why did he reject water and all the rest as the historical source, the *arché* (a word Anaximander first used to represent this kind of principle of things)? The answer to that question refers back to his picture of the universe as being the scene of constant strife. Neither water (the wet) nor any of the other stuffs (the opposites) will do as the original stuff of the universe, *precisely because* they are always warring for supremacy.

The evidence suggests that he reasoned something like this:

> Thales said that all things originated from water; but water (which we see in the form of rain, sea and rivers) is opposed to fire (the sun, the fiery aither, volcanoes, etc.) and these things are mutually destructive. How then can fire have become such a prominent part of our world, if it were from the beginning constantly opposed by the whole indefinitely extended mass of its very opposite? How, indeed, can it have appeared at all, for a single moment? (Kirk, Raven, and Schofield, 1983, p. 114)

---

*I am avoiding the word *element* here because elements in modern chemistry don't change into each other, as *arché* do. Empedocles later turned *arché* into modern elements.

That argument will work against holding any one of the four cosmic masses to be the starting place of the world insofar as they are thought of as opposites. For example, if the cold were *all* there were at the beginning of things, how did the hot manage to secure any toehold in the universe?

Monism and the *Apeiron*

Anaximander could have concluded that all four of the stuffs were equally basic, since none could have come from the others. It is important to notice that he *could have* drawn that conclusion and yet that he *did not*. Instead he *assumed* that there was only one original stuff. That assumption is called the *monistic assumption* ("mono" being "one" as in "monotheism" and "monoplane").

Anaximander must have assumed that the originative stuff must be radically different from water, fire, and the rest. It cannot be anything that lies within our experience, for if it were part of the world in that way, it would be involved in the cycle of hostility. "The warring constituents of our world, then, must have developed from a substance different from any of them—something indefinite or indeterminable" (Kirk, Raven, and Schofield, 1983, p. 114). The "primitive stuff must be neutral in the hostilities and therefore must have no definite characteristics of its own" (Guthrie, 1962, Vol. 1, p. 86).

Anaximander called this original stuff the *apeiron*. The word *peras* meant "limit" or "boundary" and "*a-*" is a mild negative prefix (as in "apolitical"), so *apeiron* means, literally, "unlimited," or "lacking limits." The *apeiron* should be understood as the unlimited, the boundless, the indefinite.

This name was chosen so as not to suggest any definite, known, sort of stuff. The existence of the *apeiron* is asserted by Anaximander wholly on the basis of argument and not on the basis of perception. As we shall see in the next chapter, that inference to something entirely outside of human experience produced a swift philosophical reaction.

Thus everything that can be said about the *apeiron* is based on inference and not on experience of it. First, the *apeiron* is not spatially infinite—the idea of spatial infinity was strange to Greek minds. Yet Anaximander thought of it as an enormous mass, indefinitely large. The *apeiron* was, however, thought to be temporally infinite, unlimited in time. He called it "eternal and ageless," "deathless and imperishable." Why does he say that it has always existed? Because if the source, the first cause, of all things had a beginning, it would itself have a source and could not be *the* source, the first cause. Hence, the *apeiron* had no beginning. (We shall see later why it is also deathless.) Furthermore, the *apeiron* must be internally undifferentiated—no line can be drawn between parts of it. It is an indistinguishable mass, and hence also unbounded in that way.

For the Greeks, the most important property of the gods, along with their power, was their immortality—the chief way in which gods differ from other things in the world. So when Anaximander says that the *apeiron* is "deathless," that reveals he is thinking of it as a *divine being*. That conception of the original stuff of the world is closely related to the connection we found in Thales between "All things are (made of) water" and "All things are full of gods." Although these thinkers were working at creating a depersonalized conception of nature, we must not think of them as attempting thereby to separate nature and religion. That move will come in due course. For Anaximander, the stuff of the world is taken to be a deity, an indestructible being, though clearly not one of the gods of ordinary religious belief.

Anaximander's Cosmogony

How did the cosmic masses, the opposites, come into being from the *apeiron?* On one point there is no doubt. Anaximander conceived of it as a process of separation. Recall that Hesiod also began the history of the world with a separation (with a division of a primordial unity into Earth and Sky). But unlike Hesiod, Anaximander thought of this first step, not as a spatial separation, but rather as a "separating out" or "separating off." What it was more precisely is in doubt. Some say that the separation was *mechanical,* caused by a vortex motion in the *apeiron* that sifted the opposites out and into their location in the universe. Others hold that the separation was thought of *biologically,* that Anaximander thought of it as the production of an egg that contained the opposites.

Guidance of the World

The *apeiron* was not all used up in the creation of the universe. What is left is out there, surrounding the perceptible cosmos, a permanent reservoir. So Anaximander supposes a fifth kind of stuff, although this material must be outside the developed universe, encircling the whole without interacting with it.

According to Aristotle, Anaximander also held that the *apeiron* "steers all things." So the *apeiron* is divine not just in being indestructible but also in being alive—capable, that is, of self-initiated change (it did, after all, produce a world out of itself)—and in possessing something like intelligence and purpose. Since the *apeiron* cannot be part of the organized world of our experience, how is it able to exercise any control over that world? What Anaximander most likely had in mind derives from his claim that the world has built into it a regulatory principle, the law that opposites shall incur retribution for their injustices. The *apeiron* that gave rise to a lawful world could be said to steer all things by having originally implanted that principle of orderly behavior in existing things.

Quite in accord with his emphasis on cyclical change *within* the universe, it also seems that Anaximander posited a larger cycle. A universe (one at a time) would be separated off from the source, then later reabsorbed back into it, and then later still another new universe would be produced by the *apeiron*, the entire process continuing in a great cycle.

Science and System

Anaximander continued his history of the universe far beyond the point where the opposites came into being from the originative stuff. In fact, some scholars have held that his real interest was less in the original step of creation than in spelling out the subsequent details of a developing universe.

He went on to discuss the formation of a continually more organized world; that is, producing a cosmogony and cosmology that included accounts of numerous astronomical, meteorological, geological, biological, and geographical phenomena. A major achievement was his idea that Thales was wrong in thinking the earth must have something to support it in space—rather, being in the middle of the cosmos, it has no reason to move in *any* direction. Again, one important kind of phenomenon that arose in the course of the world's history is living beings. Anaximander gave an account of how life had begun—living beings came from moist earth by the warming action of the sun. Even human life must have had some beginning. Anaximander said that we came from a kind of fish; that is, we arose from a preceding kind of living creature. Although this account of the origin of life is evolutionary, it is not the modern Darwinian story, since Anaximander assumed that our ancestors did not have the fish as an ancestor but emerged from it fully formed. However, the theory is like Darwin's in one respect, and is also part of Anaximander's own larger project of depersonalizing nature, in that it accounts for the existence of life, including human life, without invoking special creation.

Anaximander also gave solutions for a significant number of smaller-scale problems. He offered explanations of eclipses, lightning, and thunder. He specified the size and shape of the earth, described the arrangement of the various heavenly bodies, and estimated their relative distances from the earth, implying that the world is geometrically organized. The details of his views on these and other such matters belong to the history of science and are not relevant to the aims of this book. (Those details can be found in any comprehensive survey, such as Guthrie's.)

Two points do need to be noticed, however. First, each of his solutions to cosmological and scientific problems was integrated into his general scheme of the universe. Anaximander attempted to produce a *coherent system* of the universe. He thought that the principles that operated initially are still operating in the present universe. And that system was intended to be comprehensive, to cover the full history and present constitution of the entire universe. Although he certainly did not manage to address himself to the complete range of natural phenomena, what he aspired to was an *ideal* for others to strive to satisfy, an ideal his successors also adopted.

When we take these things into account, it seems completely reasonable to say that Anaximander was the first great thinker in the Western intellectual tradition.

ANAXIMENES

The third of the Milesians was Anaximenes *(Ann-axe-em'-en-eez)*. He is described in ancient works as a younger contemporary of Anaximander and also as a pupil and friend. His dates are uncertain: perhaps 580–500 B.C.E. He is known to have written a book (only one sentence now remains), the style of which was much more sober than Anaximander's. "The difference in style perhaps reflects a more prosaic and scientific approach on the part of Anaximenes. We hear no more of the opposites conducting a warfare like hostile powers or 'making reparation' for an 'injustice'" (Guthrie, 1962, Vol. 1, p. 115).

Typically, Anaximenes is portrayed as a fundamentally uninteresting thinker, a plodding successor to Anaximander. That is unfair: he had a significant *philosophical* insight that made a major contribution to understanding the nature of science. His philosophical outlook precluded him from writing about the cosmos as a war zone.

Criticizing the *Apeiron*

His starting point was a rejection of the *apeiron* as the source of things. I shall speculate about why he did so, offering an interpretation that makes sense of the scant evidence.

Anaximander argued that surrounding the cosmos is a previously unknown stuff, the *apeiron,* from which all the familiar materials of the world had come. It might be thought that that inference to the *apeiron* was quite scientific in that science characteristically appeals to *unperceived* things to explain perceived natural phenomena. For example, although we cannot see, smell (and so on) magnetic fields, scientists posit such fields to best explain the behavior of iron filings, needles, and such things in the vicinity of a magnet. So too with genes, atoms, and the process of natural selection: we do not perceive them with our senses, but scientists refer to them in explaining relevant natural phenomena and thereby take it that the world contains such things.

Anaximander's resort to the *apeiron* might be thought to be the same kind of move and thus a very advanced piece of science. However, his inference that the world contains such a stuff was rejected as not good science on Anaximenes' part.

The first problem is that the *apeiron* cannot ever be perceived: it is outside the organized world that includes us. Nor can it intervene in that world and leave marks or signs of its existence. In later philosophical terminology, the *apeiron* is a *transcendent object*.

The claim that a wholly undetectable something exists behind the world is troubling, and Anaximenes seems to have been troubled. His suspicions thus raised, further inquiry apparently led him to believe that Anaximander's inference to the *apeiron* is scientifically unnecessary. A good inference to unperceivable entities is one made rationally necessary by the phenomena. Certain phenomena are noticed; for example, the manner in which iron filings behave in the vicinity of magnets. Scientists then infer that there *must be* an unperceived field that produces those effects. Again, scientists find in experience a distribution of inherited characteristics that leads them to say that there *must be* something unexperienced, which can be called a *gene*, that produces that observed pattern of inheritance.

Anaximenes' question seems to have been "In order to account for the facts of the cosmos, *must* we say that there is some stuff, the *apeiron*, that lies forever outside human experience? Is Anaximander's inference *required* by the facts of the case?"

The Opposites
Why, after all, had Anaximander been led to postulate the *apeiron*? There were two reasons. First, he had not been able to imagine how one could get fire from water or water from fire, or, more generally, how any of the basic stuffs could be derived from another. Second, he assumed that there could be only one fundamental stuff.

Anaximenes also accepted the monistic assumption. Must one, though, accept the idea that the cosmic masses cannot be transformed one into the other? Anaximander had thought they could not, because he conceived of them as *opposites*. *That* assumption necessitated his postulation of some other form of matter different from them, which could therefore give birth to them.

Thus, the *apeiron* was made necessary by the assumption that the four cosmic masses were opposites. If that assumption were denied, then it would not be necessary to infer that behind the experienced world exists an additional sort of matter that can never be observed. His distaste for unperceivable objects being greater than his certainty that the world is made up of opposites, Anaximenes thus gave up the idea that the experienced world is composed of opposites. That is, he came to describe the cosmic constituents in terms that do not demand fundamental, intrinsic conflict between them.

Science and Experience
Anaximenes appears to have had a decided philosophical preference for restricting science to what is experienceable. The *apeiron* would be beyond experience, and if any way could be found around it, that route was scientifically desirable. His implicit principle—to infer unperceived entities only as a

matter of last resort—was an important advance in the Milesians' attempt to naturalize their stories of the composition and functioning of the cosmos. It was also the first shot fired in a still continuing philosophical and scientific dispute about the legitimacy of inferences to unobserved and unobservable entities and processes.

Air

Anaximenes rejected the picture of the universe as composed of warring opposites and provided instead a more prosaic account in which earth, water, air, and fire are the cosmic constituents. He could have held that all four stuffs are equally basic, but he did not. He assumed that one of them must be the source of the others, the *arché* of the cosmos. The others must then come to be by a process of transformation from the original one.

Anaximenes did not accept Thales' idea that water is the *arché* and continuing constituent of things. Why not? Perhaps because it is difficult to see how fire could be derived from water.

However, no similar difficulty arises in thinking that *air* might be able to produce those other stuffs—air seems not to destroy any of the others. Anaximenes could cite certain observations as evidence that air does undergo the requisite transformations. For example, he might say that we can see and feel atmospheric transitions of air to fire (think of the air on hot, dry days) and of air to water (days of mist and fog). Air thus seems a plausible *arché,* a replacement for Anaximander's *apeiron.*

All commentators on Anaximenes notice that he seemed to have been especially interested in the *process* by which natural transformations come about. Separation, for instance, cannot be the basic process for causing air to become the other stuffs, because separation only sorts out what is already there. If air originally contained earth and the other types of matter and they were then sorted out, then air would not be *the* original material.

Air can be denser or rarer. Moreover, when it is thick, it is full of water; when it is thin, it is hot and dry. That fact might have suggested to Anaximenes that air can be transformed into the other stuffs by the processes of thickening and thinning. Condensing air produces first water, then earth; when air is rarefied, it becomes fire.

Thickening and thinning, unlike separation, are processes that enable new forms of stuff to come into being without positing a mixture as the original stuff. Anaximenes can also say that air solves both of Thales' aims—the same stuff can be both the historical source of the universe and the continuing constituent of all things. (The *apeiron* was not capable of doing both: it is not a constituent of this world.) Hence, for Anaximenes, air is the *arché,* the stuff from which the universe originally came and that still exists in different forms in all the objects of our developed world. The process by which these natural changes come about is the reversible process of condensation and rarefaction. (It is possible to say that the process is that of *changes in density.*

Most likely, though, Anaximenes did not see the mathematical, quantitative implications of thinking of the world's substances as being one stuff at different densities.)

In other respects, air as the principle of the world played the same role as the *apeiron*. An unlimited amount of it exists from which to generate a universe. It is eternal, having no beginning and no end. Once again, the characteristic of having no end, of being immortal, meant that air was thought of as divine. It is in eternal motion, the processes of thickening and thinning naturally always going on (that being the way air is). Since air is self-moving, self-changing, Anaximenes would have thought of it as alive.

In this way, Anaximenes may have come to the idea that the basic stuff of the world is alive. But that conclusion would immediately hook his cosmological theory up with another set of ideas. The Greeks believed that *breath* and *life* are the same. The air we breathe is our life: when we stop breathing, we die, our *psyché*, our life principle, departs. Anaximenes has succeeded in identifying the *arché* of the universe with the very stuff that is the principle of life. The consequences of identifying that which animates living beings with what materially constitutes the world turned out to be extremely important to later stages in the development of Greek philosophy.

Other Scientific Problems

Anaximenes was interested in more than just the big questions about the constitution of the universe. He also worked on the same sorts of more specialized scientific problems as did Anaximander, attempting to give solutions to them in terms of his cosmological system. Although the details of his views on those matters are beyond the bounds of our interests here, it should be remarked that Anaximenes' system, within the framework laid down by Anaximander, later became the model for Ionian cosmological and scientific inquiry.

WHY PHILOSOPHERS?

Someone might very well object, "Ah, yes, the Milesians constituted a break with the mythological past and are thus the beginning of rational attempts to explain the past and the present of the universe. But why do we call them *philosophers*? Why do we study them in the history of philosophy? It is not the task of philosophers to describe the structure of the heavens, the evolution of living beings, the structure of matter, the causes of earthquakes. Yet the Milesians had precisely those aims. Surely they were *scientists*, not philosophers."

No doubt, as *we use the terms today*, the Milesians were scientists ("physicists" and "physiologers," as Aristotle called them, those who studied *physis*, "nature"), not philosophers. That is to say, the kinds of issues with which they were concerned are what we today would all agree to be scientific issues, problems to be dealt with by specialists we call *scientists*. (Some issues, such as cosmological ones, certainly have significant philosophical aspects.) The outcomes of inquiries into those kinds of phenomena are taught in courses dealing with one or another science and are not the subject matter of philosophy courses.

Some have denied that the Milesians were scientists. The grounds for that view are interesting. Obviously, the answers the Milesians gave to the questions they asked about nature were not correct. In fact, given today's science, they got nothing right about the phenomena they investigated. It has been held that the reason for that failure is that they did not practice "the scientific method"; in particular, they did not understand that one must experiment in order to understand nature. Without that method, it is claimed, we cannot say that what they did was science.

That view won't do. Over and above relying on some fictitious set of procedures called "*the* scientific method," that view makes science identical with *modern* science. Yet science *developed*. It took centuries for inquirers to hammer out the proper way(s) to study various kinds of natural phenomena. And there is no reason to think that the process is yet over. The Milesians *were* scientists, but in being the first such they had to begin the process of creating that kind of human activity.

It does not follow, however, that we should not discuss those Pre-Socratics within the history of philosophy, that we should not call them philosophers, too. We should—for several reasons:

1. The early philosophers themselves made no such distinction between science and philosophy. Nor was such a distinction clearly made before the beginning of the twentieth century. Moreover, it is still a philosophical problem as to how and how far that distinction can be maintained. Hence, if one is to know the history of philosophy, one must know that science and philosophy grew up intertwined.

2. Probably the most important part of the Milesians' activity was not their detailed views on cosmological and scientific questions, but their rejection of mythological accounts of the world and their creation of the idea of nature as something that operates in a lawful manner. Yet that idea is not a piece of science but is rather a presupposition of scientific thought. It may be stretching things to call that idea a *philosophical* result, but the label is not wholly inappropriate.

3. Philosophy is, like the sciences, a rational enterprise. Hence the beginning of rational investigations of reality is as much the beginning of philosophy as it is of science—even if the first attempts at a rationalistic view of things were concerned with what we now understand to be scientific phenomena.

4. Philosophy—once again, like science, like any field of inquiry—is a critical activity. Almost certainly Anaximander and Anaximenes made the first attempts to criticize the views of their predecessors and *thereby* obtain a better view. Such a systematic scrutiny of the views of one's predecessors

(and contemporaries) has become a central part of the activity of philosophy. Those who began that way of doing things (and the Milesians must not be thought to have done more than *begin* creating the tools of intellectual criticism) must be counted as ancestors of modern philosophy.

5. With the Milesians, philosophy as we know it had not yet begun. But we cannot understand how philosophy, how specifically *philosophical* reflections on things, did come into being unless we understand its predecessors. The first thoughts we can clearly recognize to be philosophy were in fact reactions of those Milesian attempts to explain nature. Only by seeing what such thoughts were reactions to can we understand why philosophy, as distinct from science, began when and where it did.

BIBLIOGRAPHY

Charles H. Kahn, *Anaximander and the Origins of Greek Cosmology* (New York: Columbia University Press, 1960).

4

XENOPHANES

The historical sequence of Thales, Anaximander, and Anaximenes is very tidy, and the story flows naturally from one to the other. For the next three figures, however, the storyteller must decide what order to use. A reader who consults the various surveys of Pre-Socratic philosophy will find most of the mathematically possible orders used. My own choice is to speak first of Xenophanes, then of Pythagoras and his followers, and last of Heraclitus. My plan of organization, like all the others, has both advantages and disadvantages.

After Anaximenes, some major changes occurred in the philosophical world. For one, philosophy expanded geographically. It was no longer confined to Miletus and soon not even to Asia Minor. (That is true no matter which of the next three philosophers one chooses to discuss first.) The continuity of philosophical thought can best be seen by beginning with Xenophanes *(Zen-off'-en-eez)*.

Although not a Milesian, Xenophanes was an Ionian Greek, from Colophon, less than 50 miles north of Miletus. Born about 570 B.C.E. (which makes him about ten years younger than Anaximenes), he left Colophon shortly after it was absorbed into the Persian empire in 546 B.C.E. He migrated to the western Greek colonies (modern Italy), though he did not settle in one spot. Rather, he traveled about western Greece for the remainder of his long life (he died about 470 B.C.E.), reciting his poetry. Xenophanes was famous for (among other things) inventing a new type of satiric poetry. One consequence of his fame is that, compared to the Milesians at least, we possess a good amount of his writings—about 118 lines.

With Xenophanes, philosophy acquired some new concerns and even some new functions. Unlike his predecessors, Xenophanes was not what later came to be called a "natural philosopher." That is, he was not chiefly concerned with discovering explanations of natural phenomena or with solving cosmological problems. Do not be misled: He was quite knowledgeable about, and deeply influenced by, the Milesians' outlook and their work. But, on the whole, he was not himself an original contributor to the cosmological investigations begun by his predecessors.

To say it again, Xenophanes was basically a poet. However, much of what he wrote about was not the usual stuff of poetry—not love, war, friends, feelings, happenings. He seems rather to have been interested in the accounts of the world that his Milesian neighbors had been producing. In consequence, a good deal of his poetry dealt with natural phenomena and cosmology. Because the rationalistic outlook of the Milesians had shaped his own thinking, his poetry spread the new view and ideas to a much wider audience than their originators could reach.

XENOPHANES AND RELIGION

If all that Xenophanes had done were to educate the Greeks in the new intellectual movement, he would receive only a footnote in the history of philosophy. His major contribution was something quite different. In cosmology and in explanations of natural phenomena (such as earthquakes), the Milesians had attempted to substitute natural causes and processes for anthropomorphic conceptions. But they did not say anything about the gods of popular belief. Zeus and the rest were simply not mentioned in the new-style explanations. Xenophanes' chief importance is that he worked out the *religious* implications of Ionian cosmology.

The evidence suggests that Xenophanes criticized the common conception of the gods in three different ways. He seems to have recognized that the gods of ordinary Greek religion were believed in, at least in part, because they provided explanations of natural phenomena. Against the background of Ionian thought, however, they were not necessary for that purpose. Lightning, for example, has a natural explanation, so the idea of an anthropomorphic deity hurling thunderbolts in anger is unnecessary. See Fragment 32 about the rainbow: "She whom men call Iris, she too is a cloud, purple, red and yellow to sight." Xenophanes also realized (what was fairly obvious) that the Homeric gods were morally undesirable beings: "Homer and Hesiod have attributed to the gods everything that, among men, is shameful and reproachful: stealing, adultery, mutual deceit" (Fragment 11).

The third line of criticism is the most remarkable. Xenophanes noticed that different peoples project their own racial characteristics (and probably more) onto their gods. "Ethiopians think of their gods as black and snub-nosed, Thracians think of theirs as having gray-blue eyes and red hair" (Fragment 16). Of course, it is possible to conclude from the observation of that cultural relativity that the Homeric gods were created, racially and probably socially, in the image of the Greeks. But Xenophanes came to a much more radical conclusion, namely, that the gods of all peoples are created in the image of *humanity:*

But if oxen and horses and lions had hands and could draw as man
does, horses would draw the gods shaped like horses and oxen like
oxen, each making the bodies of the gods like their own. (Fragment 15)
    Mortals think that the gods are born and have clothes and speech
and bodies like their own. (Fragment 14)

The Greek gods had become unnecessary for explanatory purposes,
they were not morally desirable beings anyway, and they were a picture of
those who believed in them. For those reasons, they had to go. But much
more broadly, there is no reason, Xenophanes concluded, to believe that any
divine being is humanlike. Such beliefs being but a matter of human fiction,
all anthropomorphic gods must be surrendered.

In one way, Xenophanes continued a main theme of the earlier Milesian
activity. His predecessors had worked at depersonalizing nature. Xenophanes carried that attack a step further by criticizing personalized conceptions of the divine. The philosophical tradition acquired thereby not
only a new problem, the nature of the divine, but also an entirely new function: criticism of institutions, cultural criticism.

XENOPHANES' GOD

Xenophanes rejected any conception of divine beings that made them out to
be humanlike and morally imperfect. And when he said "mortals think that
the gods are born," he surely meant that it is a mistake to think that anything
divine could have come into being. It follows that, for Xenophanes, the
proper conception of the divine involves denying that the gods have any
specifically human qualities while holding them to be both uncreated (and
of course deathless) and morally good.

Did Xenophanes believe that there is anything answering to that conception? That is, did he believe that there is some truly divine being
or beings? Yes. He found just such a being implied by the Ionian cosmologies.
The Milesians had thought of the basic stuff of the universe as uncreated and
imperishable. And that meant, for the Greeks, that the stuff was divine. In
those ideas, Xenophanes found a legitimate god: "One god, greatest among
gods and men, in no way like mortals in body or in mind" (Fragment 23).

Although that passage literally implies more than one god, the best
ancient evidence suggests that Xenophanes thought that only one god
exists; that he held (even if flexibly) a monotheistic view.

Undoubtedly the Milesian cosmologies had suggested this replacement
for the pantheon of popular gods Xenophanes had rejected. His philosophical predecessors, themselves obviously not much interested in religion, had
held there to be one basic stuff that was everlasting (divine) and self-moving,
self-changing (alive). Here was a suitable deity, certainly not an anthropomorphic being.

There is some reason to believe that Xenophanes (perhaps somewhat fuzzily) departed from the Milesians to hold that the cosmos (the universe) is divine, rather than the stuff out of which the cosmos is made. If so, he cannot have thought that the general structure of the world came into being as the Milesians had held—he had already said that gods cannot be born. Furthermore, if the cosmos is the god and thus imperishable, there cannot be successive world orders or universes, as Anaximander had claimed.

The universe exhibits a pattern of justice and equality between its constituents (see Anaximander), a pattern that arises from its *physis* (its nature). Therefore, such a cosmic morality satisfies Xenophanes' requirement that a proper god be morally good. This conclusion is quite independent of whether the cosmos or its material parts constitute the god of Xenophanes.

We have some evidence about further features of this god. Fragment 23 (quoted earlier) implies that it has both a body and a mind, though of course not at all like those of humans. It seems that Xenophanes held the universe—the deity—to be spherical. The god possesses mental powers (thought and perception are mentioned in the fragments), so the cosmos is not only alive but conscious.

One of Xenophanes' accomplishments was the articulation of a completely new *type* of divine being. In identifying the universe as the sole true divinity, he introduced what later came to be called "the god of the philosophers" into Western thought. Here was a god very different from those recognized by typical religious belief. This deity could be worshiped, although probably not prayed to. The idea of rituals, of all cultish organization and behavior, is quite inappropriate for the type of god introduced by Xenophanes. (For an excellent discussion of related issues, see the essay by Vlastos mentioned in the Bibliography at the end of this chapter.)

KNOWLEDGE

Xenophanes pushed the philosophical tradition forward not by further cosmological refinements but by extending the application of rationality and naturalism to another issue, the nature of the divine. He was an innovator in yet another area: he reflected on the nature of knowledge, thereby introducing into philosophy yet another topic, which was later to become of crucial importance. Xenophanes was thus the creator of two subareas of philosophy: (1) *rational theology*, the attempt to establish the existence and attributes of deity by rational means; and (2) *epistemology*, the study of the nature of knowledge.

Xenophanes said, "The gods have not revealed all things to men from the beginning: but by seeking men find out better in time" (Fragment 18). Our information about the divine does not come from revelation. We learn by investigation—and since the universe is the deity, we acquire our understanding of the chief god by pursuing those inquiries into nature that were inaugurated by the Milesians.

Fragment 18 implies that humanity makes progress in understanding. That idea became very important in Greek thought in the century following Xenophanes, and he may well have been the first to express it. (The standard Greek conception was that human life as then known was in a state of decline from an earlier golden age.)

But does that progress in understanding amount to *knowledge?* Xenophanes thought it did not: "No man knows or ever will know the truth about the gods and about everything of which I speak. For even if someone were, by chance, to speak the whole truth, he would not *know* it—in all things there is opinion" (Fragment 34). Scientific investigations lead to an improvement in our understanding of the world. But we thereby only acquire better *beliefs,* not genuine knowledge.

Why did Xenophanes think that knowledge, at least scientific knowledge, shall elude us? The relativity of sense perception is probably a main reason. See Fragment 38: "If God had not made yellow honey, men would think figs to be sweet." That is, what we can say about the world—even in the most favored case, that of perception—is a function of our circumstances and not simply based on how the world *is.*

Xenophanes not only introduced the issue of knowledge into the history of thought, but he also introduced the important distinction between knowledge and belief. Moreover, in holding that we shall have only belief and never knowledge (in science, at least), Xenophanes began the development of *skepticism,* the view that knowledge is impossible. Skepticism, however, had little immediate impact:

> After the dogmatism of the Milesians (and also of Pythagoras, mocked by Xenophanes . . . for his extravagant theory . . .) an appeal to caution was salutary, and from this time on there was certainly more verbal reference to the broadest aspects of epistemology. But Xenophanes' revival of the traditional doctrine of human limitations, this time in a partly philosophical context, did little else that is noticeable to curb the naturally over-dogmatic tendency of Greek philosophy in its first buoyant stages. (Kirk, Raven, and Schofield, 1983, p. 181)

It was only later that serious and systematic inquiry began about whether *knowledge* of the history and behavior of the natural world is possible.

BIBLIOGRAPHY

Gregory Vlastos, "Theology and Philosophy in Early Greek Thought," reprinted in R. E. Allen and David J. Furley, eds., *Studies in Pre-Socratic Philosophy,* Vol. 1 (London: Routledge & Kegan Paul, 1975).

5

PYTHAGORAS AND THE PYTHAGOREANS

The ancient sources are quite definite in saying that Pythagoras *(Pie-thag' -oras)* was a major *religious* teacher and reformer. Moreover, it is certain that he founded a religious order devoted to his teachings. The question that has divided scholars is whether he should *also* be counted a philosopher-scientist, as falling within those general developments begun in Miletus. The brotherhood he established produced, during the course of its history, a good deal of philosophical and scientific work. Thus the only genuine question is whether its founder, Pythagoras himself, was an originator of philosophical and scientific thought and activity.

Here I shall presume that he should be counted among the Pre-Socratic philosophers. It is difficult to think otherwise, even though direct evidence is not available. Guthrie notes, "His character as one of the most original thinkers in history, a founder of mathematical science and philosophical cosmology, although not directly attested by such early and impregnable sources, must be assumed as the only reasonable explanation of the unique impression made by his name on subsequent thought. It was both as religious teacher and as scientific genius that he was from his own lifetime and for many centuries afterwards venerated by his followers, violently attacked by others, but ignored by none" (Guthrie, 1962, Vol. 1, p. 181). (For an account of Pythagoras based on the opposite assessment of his personal contribution, see Barnes, 1979, Vol. 1, Chapter 6.)

The problem that remains, once we have made this assumption, is to try to understand how the two sides of his (and of his followers') thought, the religious and the philosophical, were connected.

A NEW PHILOSOPHICAL MOVEMENT

Before discussing his views, we can make a broad generalization about how Pythagoras' religious and philosophical views were linked. Pythagoras was fundamentally a religious teacher whose chief interest was in the "right way of life." He conceived the right way to live as involving the establishment of the proper relationship between a person and the universe. But to say that the proper relationship between person and world is "such-and-such" is precisely to have some ideas about what the universe is like. Hence, from his religious concerns derives an interest in philosophical and scientific matters.

Although Pythagoras was, in part, a continuation of the intellectual tradition begun in Miletus, he also and more importantly brought radically new interests and new ideas into philosophy. His concern with cosmological and other scientific problems was harnessed to his religious concerns. His predecessors had not started from a fundamentally religious outlook and interest. The chief motive for the Ionians' philosophizing had been curiosity about the universe and its workings, coupled with a dissatisfaction with the existing mythological mode of representing nature. They thought that understanding the universe correctly is something desirable in itself. Pythagoras, however, sought to understand the world in order to get in harmony with it.

Out of those differences grew the two main traditions in Greek philosophical thought. The "Ionian" outlook derives from Thales and Anaximander, while the "Italian" side of Greek philosophy began with Pythagoras. The fundamental difference involved differing conceptions of what someone is doing when engaging in inquiry, of whether philosophy is a spiritual activity or not.

PYTHAGORAS' LIFE

Born about 570 B.C.E., Pythagoras was a native of the island of Samos, which lies just off the coast from Miletus. He left Samos, perhaps because of political and moral disagreements with its ruler, around 530 B.C.E., presumably well acquainted with the new modes of thinking that had been developed by the neighboring Milesians. He migrated to Croton, an important Greek settlement on the east coast of southern Italy.

At Croton, Pythagoras rather quickly gathered a circle of disciples around himself (no doubt he was a very impressive, charismatic man). He and this group, the original Pythagoreans, soon became the major political power in Croton and before long dominated other communities in the area. Around the end of the century, a rebellion occurred against their rule. Some Pythagoreans were killed; others fled, including Pythagoras himself. He died shortly thereafter, about 495 B.C.E.

Pythagoras became a legendary figure for the Greeks, a man to whom miracles were imputed, a man of great wisdom, a man dedicated to *historie,* inquiry, and proper living. We know nothing of him personally. The many stories that have come down to us are traditional tales, not fact.

THE PYTHAGOREANS

The brotherhood Pythagoras founded at Croton continued in existence for nearly two hundred years, finally vanishing about 330 B.C.E. The rebellion that preceded Pythagoras' death did not end the power of the Pythagoreans in southern Italy. An even more extensive revolt about 450 B.C.E. did succeed in breaking their political domination, causing them to scatter over all of Greece, banded together in small groups. For the remaining hundred-plus years of the society's existence, they were not geographically united.

The Pythagoreans were not just a group of friends and admirers of Pythagoras. They were members of an organized sect that had initiation rites, secret lore, and rules of behavior (chiefly various prohibitions against certain kinds of food and dress). Whatever philosophical work was done by the Pythagoreans was undertaken as part of a religious life and was carried out within the framework of the brotherhood.

DIFFICULTIES OF EXPOSITION

It is difficult to produce a satisfactory account of Pythagorean philosophy. The Pythagorean outlook, insofar as we can grasp it, was powerful and crude at the same time, a mixture of high sophistication, great confusion on some topics, primitive superstition, and a complex pattern of motivation and thought that today we find very difficult to comprehend.

Moreover, there are extensive problems of evidence, troubles over and above the typical shortage of reliable historical records. Here we have more than one individual thinker to contend with: we have both Pythagoras himself and the various Pythagoreans who came after him. And it is even worse than that. Because the Pythagorean society existed for two hundred years and because for much of that time its members were geographically separated, it is certain that Pythagorean doctrine underwent growth and development and was also subject to differences of opinion and interpretation. Consequently, more than one set of Pythagorean doctrines arose. Furthermore, precisely because this articulation and extension of Pythagoras' views was undertaken within a religious order, ideas developed later in the tradition tended to be attributed to the master, a practice making it difficult to sort out who contributed what ideas and when. That is especially serious because there is no record of Pythagoras having *written* anything. Last, Pythagorean doctrines were secret to the initiates of the sect, and the sect was very good at not revealing its mysteries. Not until about 400 B.C.E. did the first extensive break in the secrecy occur. All these complications explain why so many scholarly disputes have arisen about how to treat Pythagoras and his followers. It should also indicate why the attribution of any given view to Pythagoras himself is quite chancy.

Nonetheless, I will discuss Pythagorean ideas. In the interests of economy, I will tell only one story; it is possible to divide the whole into several distinct but related stories. I am blurring distinctions not only between Pythagoras and the Pythagoreans but also between sixth-century ideas and important developments in Pythagoreanism that took place about 450 B.C.E.

DEVELOPMENTS IN RELIGION

An examination of Pythagoras (and his followers) must begin with his religious teaching. Pythagoras was associated with innovations in religious belief and practice. He did not spring up as an isolated figure. His innovations were (an important) part of a more general set of religious developments in the Greek world. (In fact, new religions were the order of that day: Buddha, 543–483 B.C.E., and Confucius, 551–479(?) B.C.E., were Pythagoras' exact contemporaries.)

For a variety of reasons, the "official" religion, the Homeric religion that celebrated the gods of Olympus, was becoming less satisfactory to a significant number of Greeks in the time of Pythagoras. (For the "sociology" of those developments, see the Cornford reference in the Bibliography at the end of this chapter.) One major source of increasing dissatisfaction with the official religion was the wide gulf between humans and the gods. Despite the all-too-human character of the Homeric gods, that likeness of human and divine natures was nonetheless sharply limited. Being a god was one thing; being a human was quite another. One was immortal, and the other was not. In consequence, a characteristic feature of the new developments was some form of *assimilation* of the human to the divine. Xenophanes, Pythagoras' contemporary, shared the dissatisfaction with the existing condition of religious belief. His response to it, however, was not at all in the same direction as the developments we are now discussing. Xenophanes' religious innovations had to do with the nature of divine beings; Pythagoras' innovations dealt with the nature and fate of the soul.

The religious practices that arose in support of the theme of uniting human and god were various. Typically, these were embodied in a cult. These cults were organized so that an individual, following a period of preparation, was initiated into the system of beliefs and activities, a process that included a revelation of the mysteries. In such a fashion, the initiate was joined to the god. A striking movement called Orphism (from the legendary singer Orpheus) added to those features the practice of daily religious exercises, chiefly, the avoidance of certain activities.

Pythagoras' religious views cannot be fully disentangled from Orphism. Fundamental similarities exist between the two groups (although there is also one major difference concerning the role of inquiry). It cannot be settled whether the Orphic material was used by Pythagoras or whether the Orphics learned from Pythagoras. (On Orphism, see the references at the end of the chapter.)

CENTRAL RELIGIOUS DOCTRINES

One of Pythagoras' central religious doctrines was that of the transmigration of the soul, that is, the belief that the soul would be incarnated in a different body (or bodies) at some time following death (following the end of the present incarnation). Moreover, he held that a person could be reincarnated in the bodies of other kinds of animals, birds as well as beasts. Clearly, one who holds such a view will also think that humans and other animals are closely related. One consequence of believing in that kinship comes out in the central prohibition of the Pythagorean community: one must not eat animal flesh.

It would be possible to believe that a soul goes through several incarnations while also believing that it will eventually perish. Pythagoras, however, also taught that the soul is immortal.

To think of the soul as immortal, as Pythagoras did, involved more than simply having a new belief about the soul. That new belief was connected with a fundamental change in the conception of a soul. The Greek term *psuché*, transliterated into English as *psyché*, is often translated as "soul." However, it would be more accurately translated as "principle of life" or as "animating force," at least in the centuries with which we are concerned. That is, when a person had died and the corpse was left motionless, it could be said that the *psyché* had departed and mean by that no more than "the thing has lost its powers of animation, is now incapable of moving itself." No *theory* about the *psyché* need be involved in such a remark. Yet the Homeric poems show a rough theory about the *psyché*: it is thought to survive death (though immortality is definitely not suggested), and in surviving it is thought to retain some measure of personal identity. That is, Hector's *psyché* survives his death with at least some of Hector's memories, fears, hopes, character traits, and so on.

Despite the notion of survival in the Homeric poems, what is most notable is how little interest in such survival is shown by both the poet and the heroes:

> In Homer too the *psyche* survived after death, but that brought no
> consolation to his heroes. The *psyche* by itself was the merest simu-
> lacrum of the man, lacking strength and wits, both of which it owed
> to its association with the body. . . . This was a natural creed for men
> of a heroic age, who equated the goodness of life with bodily prowess
> in battle, feasting and love. The real self was the body. Death meant
> separation from the body, and hence from life in any sense which
> these robust fighters could appreciate. (Guthrie, 1962, Vol. 1, p. 196)

With Pythagoras, the *psyché* has clearly been greatly elevated in importance, and not just because he had declared it immortal. Earlier, in talking of Anaximander and Anaximenes, I noted that the Greeks held that what is immortal is divine. Hence Pythagoras, in holding the human soul to be immortal, was in effect declaring its divinity—a striking way of accomplishing the assimilation of human and god. The consequence, then, of believing in immortality was to put a wholly new value on the *psyché*, to alter its importance in both human life and the universe.

Conversely, the human body and its functions (among those functions were "prowess in battle, feasting and love") fell sharply in value, compared with the *psyché,* for the Pythagoreans. This radical re-estimation of the relative worth of those different aspects of the human being was no doubt rooted in those social changes that had produced a way of life in Pythagoras' time that was vastly different from the heroic life.

For Pythagoras and those who were inclined to his religious views, belief in the immortality of the *psyché* was far from sufficient to satisfy their religious longings. Unlike the Homeric heroes, those who wished for union with the gods would feel life on this earth, at least the normal patterns of life, to be sadly inadequate and dissatisfying. Given such an attitude, the prospect of reincarnation was quite dismal, especially if reincarnations were to go on *forever,* as the doctrine of immortality suggests. Consequently, Pythagoras held out the possibility of breaking out of the cycle of incarnations and thereby achieving full assimilation to the divine.

The first matter to understand must be why there are continuing incarnations. The answer is that the soul is placed in a body (which now must be thought of as something like a prison) as punishment for corruption and wrongdoing. Hence, what is necessary to secure release from future births is *purification* (or *catharsis,* in both Greek and English) to wipe away the stains of corruption. Although all the religious developments with which Pythagoras was associated made purification a central aim of life, they differed as to the means or techniques of becoming purified. (About Pythagoras' views on that topic there is a good deal to say, but it is best said somewhat later.)

Reincarnation is the doctrine that *one and the same* soul animates a sequence of bodies. What happens, however, after the final incarnation of a given *psyché* when, having attained purity, freedom from further punishment is achieved? Does the individual *psyché* continue? We don't know what the Pythagoreans thought. If they regarded the *psyché* as an *entity* (much as the *psychés* in Homer), then they might think the purified soul would continue to exist savoring the bliss of escape from the pain of incarnated existence as well as other delights. However, they might have "believed that *psyché,* 'life,' was somehow a unity, a single mass, a part of which was scattered in an impure form throughout the world, while another part, into which the individual soul would be reabsorbed after its final reincarnation, retained its purity" (Kirk and Raven, 1960, p. 224). To so lose one's individuality might be the ultimate assimilation of human to god.

People who are somewhat familiar with different religious systems are struck by the similarity between Pythagoras' doctrines and those of other systems, particularly the Indian (though later we will also see likenesses to the Chinese and the Persian). Those likenesses become more striking when we realize that the set of views just discussed were new to Greece in the sixth century B.C.E. The question inevitably arises: Were there outside—that is, non-Greek—influences on Pythagoras and/or the Orphic movement?

The answer can only be that despite the wealth of ancient stories about Pythagoras' travels, we don't know; we have no clear evidence one way or the other.

THE PYTHAGOREAN STYLE OF PURIFICATION: FROM RELIGION TO PHILOSOPHY

The account of Pythagoreanism so far has mentioned nothing especially philosophical. Up to this point, the Pythagoreans have been described as a religious sect, seemingly not more worthy of inclusion in a book on the history of Greek philosophy than any of several other Greek religious groups. What does make them something more than just another cult and makes them part of the development of Greek philosophy is the particular version of purification we can attribute to Pythagoras.

Various combinations of techniques were employed by cults in producing that state of purity necessary to achieve the union of human and god: initiation rites, revelations, taboos to be observed, orgiastic practices. The Pythagoreans used those same techniques, but Pythagoras added to them something highly unique—call it theorizing (*theoria*) or inquiry (*historie*). In short, what was philosophically distinctive about the religious teaching of Pythagoras was the idea that *intellectual activity* is an important part of the process of achieving salvation.

Our word "philosophy" comes from the Greek *philosophia*, which meant "love of wisdom." It has been claimed that Pythagoras was the first to call himself a *philosophos*, a lover of wisdom, a philosopher. That may not be true, but it *is* true that the Pythagoreans attempted to appropriate the word for their own set of interests and views. That marked the beginning of two conflicting conceptions of philosophy that have persisted through the centuries: one view regards philosophy as a quasi-science, a conception deriving ultimately from the Milesians; the other, first propounded by Pythagoras, thinks that there is some special connection between philosophy and religion, that philosophy is a spiritual enterprise.

THE SUBJECT MATTER OF PYTHAGOREAN INQUIRY

What were the Pythagoreans' philosophical interests? The first answer must be general enough to show why Pythagoras could posit an intimate connection between theorizing and religious salvation.

The Milesians had come to think that natural objects interact and change in orderly ways rather than whimsically or as consequences of unpredictable humanlike passions. They had attempted to investigate these regularities, some hidden, some fairly obvious. The word *kosmos*, as I mentioned earlier, was shifting in meaning: originally meaning "order" or "arrangement" in general, it was now coming to refer to one particular order, that displayed in the natural world, an order best exemplified visibly by the behavior of the heavenly bodies. The word would soon come to mean "the world"; that is, the *kosmos* would be the universe conceived of as an orderly entity. The primary answer to the question of what the Pythagoreans studied is that they, like the Milesians, inquired into the order of things, into the arrangement of the cosmos.

But how did that process assist one's soul? Pythagoras seems to have thought that to discover and contemplate order in things produces order in the inquirer's *psyché* (a doctrine that, later, will be central to Plato's *Republic*).

A somewhat more full account of his probable train of thought would go something like this: The activity and organization of the world is, despite appearances, characterized by order. Because the *psyché* tends to take on the characteristics of—tends to become *like*—its surroundings, investigating and contemplating the patterns and arrangements of the world and its objects will cause the soul to become attuned to that order, that is, to become like it, orderly. (This process of reducing the chaos and confusion in ourselves, in contemporary terms of "getting our act together," is presumably what purification is. Later, Plato also believed that *moral* corruption would be canceled by *psychic harmony*.) But the world, as the philosophical tradition had agreed, is divine. Hence, to the extent that we are able to copy in our *psychés*, through inquiry, the system of order found in the world, we will be godlike. When the *psyché* is finally functioning in complete harmony with the world and with itself, we shall break free of the cycle of incarnations and permanently be one with the world, with god.

Mathematics

That the Pythagoreans took the universe to be rationally arranged and that their inquiries sought to reveal that order shows them to be intellectual descendants of the Milesians. Nonetheless, they differed very significantly from their predecessors not only in their religious motivation for inquiry but also in the kind of theory about the cosmos they produced.

To begin to grasp the nature of that difference, we must start from the fact that ever since antiquity Pythagoras and the Pythagoreans have been famous for their contributions to mathematics.

Thales was said to have brought geometry from Egypt to the Greeks. And, given his connection with Babylonian astronomy, he must have been at least conversant with the sophisticated arithmetical tools used by the Babylonians. Whether or not Thales was responsible for initiating those developments, it is clear that mathematics began to flourish in Ionia in the sixth century B.C.E.

Pythagoras, born in Ionia, no doubt acquired a knowledge of that young mathematical tradition as well as of Milesian science before he migrated west. There is some reason to believe that Pythagoras not only imparted a dedication to mathematics to his disciples but also was a great mathematician himself. For instance, it *may* have been Pythagoras (not just some later follower) who discovered that theorem that still bears his name. The Pythagorean theorem states that the square of the hypotenuse is equal to the sum of the squares of the other sides of a right triangle ($a^2 = b^2 + c^2$). No matter what his personal role in mathematics, there is no doubt that later Pythagoreans made substantial contributions to mathematics.

The Pythagoreans, however, did not engage in mathematical inquiry (simply) because they found it intellectually fascinating. For them, pursuing mathematical truth was part of the right way of life—was a religious activity. They probably thought of mathematics as spiritually uplifting in two respects. The first begins with the fact that the Greeks came to conceive of mathematics quite differently from the way other peoples had thought of and practiced it:

> The Egyptians had thought of geometry as a matter of individual rect-
> angular or triangular fields. The Greek lifts it from the plane of the
> concrete and material and begins to think about rectangles and tri-
> angles themselves, which have the same properties whether they are
> embodied in fields of several acres or in pieces of wood or cloth a few
> inches long, or simply represented by lines drawn in the sand. In fact
> their material embodiment ceases to be of any importance. . . . [The
> Greek discovery of form] marks the advance from percepts to concepts,
> from the individual examples perceived by sight or touch to the univer-
> sal notion which we conceive in our minds—in sculpture, no longer an
> individual man but the ideal of humanity; in geometry, no longer tri-
> angles but the nature of triangularity and the consequences which logi-
> cally and necessarily flow from being a triangle. (Guthrie, 1962, Vol. 1,
> pp. 36–37)

The Greeks were beginning to make what turned out to be a central philosophical distinction. It was becoming clear that different kinds of inquiry exist. Especially, there is a difference between *empirical* matters that we learn through the use of our senses and by our experience (such as that a particular piece of wood is a square measuring 2 by 2 units) and matters that are *logically necessary* and not known on the basis of perception and experience (such as that a square must have four sides and that $2 + 2 = 4$).

The Pythagoreans may well have played a role in recognizing that distinction and in realizing that mathematics is an abstract, deductive inquiry that deals with *necessities,* but what is crucial here is that those insights fitted very nicely into their religious views. The various "material embodiments" of mathematical objects are not mathematically important; the principles *behind* those "embodiments" are the subject of mathematics. Those principles, the mathematical truths, are not discovered by the senses, by bodily organs, but by the mind, by the *psyché.* Hence, because in mathematics we are studying, say, triangularity and not particular triangles and because mathematical knowledge is a function of the intellectual powers of the *psyché* and not a function of the senses, in studying mathematics we are learning to distance ourselves from bodies, especially our own, and so are helping ourselves secure freedom from the body.

Mathematics was thought to be a spiritual enterprise also in a second respect. Mathematics was understood to be an abstract, theoretical discipline in its own right; nonetheless, its principles *are* embodied in the world around us. We use the mathematical truth that $2 + 2 = 4$ to calculate that a particular piece of wood measuring 2 inches by 2 inches has an area of 4 square inches. The Pythagoreans held that mathematics is the key to revealing and understanding patterns of order in the world of experience, those patterns the contemplation of which could shape the soul in their orderly likeness.

Music, Mathematics, and the Soul

It is a characteristic Pythagorean view that the fundamental regularities of the perceptible world are mathematical in nature. In all likelihood, the Pythagoreans were led to that view by a spectacular discovery concerning music, a discovery that can plausibly be attributed to Pythagoras himself.

Three musical intervals formed the basis of the Greek musical system: the octave, the fourth, and the fifth. Pythagoras (?) discovered that those intervals, those perceptible but recurring differences between sounds, are a function of fixed numerical ratios. For instance, to produce notes an octave apart on vibrating strings adjusted to the same tension, one string must be precisely twice as long as the other. Only the 2:1 ratio will produce notes an octave apart. Similarly, a string will produce notes a fifth above another string when and only when their lengths stand in a 3:2 ratio—and one note is a fourth above another only if the ratio of the lengths of the plucked strings is 4:3.

Here was a hidden piece of order in the universe that could only be grasped *numerically*. If the recognition and contemplation of order is good for the soul, then the discovery of these musical ratios is proof that mathematics must be studied and employed in the proper way of life.

Music, Number, and the Cosmos

Pythagoras seems to have drawn several conclusions from that initial grasp of the mathematics of music. It confirmed a belief in a lawful universe and clarified how mathematics could be thought of as a spiritual enterprise. The discovery also led to a belief in the mystical significance of the number 10. The ratios involved were 2:1, 3:2, and 4:3. That is, they are constructed of the first four integers. But the sum of those 4 integers $(1 + 2 + 3 + 4)$ is 10. Hence (!) 10 contains within itself all the powers of the basic phenomena. It must not be forgotten that the Pythagoreans were enthusiasts as well as mathematicians and mathematical physicists. They dealt in numerology as much as in number theory and indeed saw no difference between the two.

The most important suggestion gleaned from the discovery was an idea about how to regard the constitution of the world. The Milesians too had thought of the world as a rationally ordered entity despite the variety of things existing within it and the variety of changes those things undergo. The *arché,* the originating principle, of such an order seemed to them to reside in the existence of some stuff that lay behind all things and persisted through change. The musical discovery suggested to Pythagoras a wholly new *kind* of answer to that question about the foundation of the world's order.

What is the central feature of the musical scale? Surely not the strings. As long as the ratios are preserved, the strings can be of any length and can be made of any vibrating material. Nor need a string even be involved: notes at those intervals can be produced on a wind instrument, say, a flute. The only requirement is that the columns of air in the instrument should stand to each other in the proper ratios. Given such facts, it seemed clear to the Pythagoreans that the principle involved does not concern the *stuff* out of which notes are produced. Rather, what is vital are the *ratios* lying behind the production of the notes. The *arché* of the scale is *numerical.*

Pythagoras and his followers appear to have leaped from the musical case to a general answer concerning the whole of the universe. What is the *arché* of the cosmos? Number. The world is not unified by being composed of some kind of stuff that transforms itself into various forms and things. Its constitution is numerical: proportions and ratios and numbers are the "stuff" of the world.

Form, Matter, and Reality

Devising that account of the principle of things, and doing so in opposition to the Milesian type of account, initiated some persistent philosophical disputes. For instance, it raised a question as to how science ought to be done: Should scientific descriptions and explanations be mathematical or not?

Connected with that issue, but more general, is a philosophical debate about the nature of things, about what is ultimately real. That debate emerged out of a distinction that can be used to characterize the differences between the Milesians and the Pythagoreans as to what the *arché* of the world is. The contrast is that between *form* and *matter.*

Pythagoreans talked of the world and its objects as constituted by ratios, by mathematical formulas that specify the *structural* properties that make something what it is. This numerical account of things was later generalized by descendants of the Pythagoreans, chiefly Plato, to the idea that it is the form of a thing, and not what it is made of, that makes it the kind of thing it is. Mice and men, toothpicks and tables, differ not (ultimately at least) in the materials out of which they are constructed but in the organization of that matter, in their shapes.

It would be very misleading to think of the Milesians as "materialists" and the Pythagoreans as "formalists." Those terms have overtones that were not possible in the sixth century B.C.E. In fact, the Pythagorean answer to the question of the *arché* of things was only the occasion for philosophers to *begin* to get clear about what the distinction between form and matter is. As we shall see next, the distinction was certainly not completely clear to the Pythagoreans themselves.

Things Are Numbers

Preliminary warning: The views I attribute to the Pythagoreans in this and the next section were held by Aristotle to be genuinely Pythagorean. Recent scholarship is inclined to doubt that Aristotle was correct on this point. Nonetheless, I shall be conservative and include the topic here.

In their enthusiasm for understanding the world quantitatively, the Pythagoreans held not only that the cosmos is *organized* mathematically but also that it is *made* of numbers. This view, that things *are* numbers, was held by Aristotle to be important to the Pythagorean account of the history and nature of the universe.

Despite its significance for them, the idea that things can be constructed out of numbers is the outcome of several pieces of confusion. Those confusions, however, are intelligible in the historical context. It is obvious to us (and was obvious by the time of Plato) that the organization of a thing and its material elements are wholly different *kinds* of feature. The recognition that there is a clear distinction came only after considerable philosophical reflection. Again, it is clear that numbers are *logically* quite different kinds of thing from pieces of stuff. The number 4, for example, (necessarily) cannot be cut, moved, weighted, given a spatial location, measured, nailed, glued, and so on, but objects, things, *can* be dealt with thus. Therefore, it is logically odd to think that a spatial object might be *constructed out of* nonspatial "entities" such as numbers. But it is not strange that the Pythagoreans failed to realize that; that realization was achieved only in consequence of philosophical criticism of their position.

Another source of confusion is language. Just what is wrong with the following argument? "The box is $2 \times 2 \times 2$; $2 \times 2 \times 2$ is 8; therefore the box *is* 8 (the number 8)." A great deal of post-Pythagorean philosophical effort was needed to work out the differences in the use of the word "is" in the sentences "That thing is 2×2" and "2×2 is 4" so that today we can understand why it is illegitimate to draw the Pythagorean conclusion "hence that thing is a number."

The Representation of Numbers

Scholars are agreed that over and above the lack of philosophical distinctions available to them, one further special historical reason lies behind the Pythagoreans' belief that things are numbers. Not having an abstract system of numerical notation, such as the Arabic "1," "2," "3," or the Roman "I," "II," "III," the Pythagoreans represented numbers by objects, such as pebbles or dots, arranged into geometrical figures. (Think of how we still represent numbers on dice, and of how we speak of unemployment *figures* when we mean "the number of unemployed.") They wrote the (sacred) number 10 thus:

$$
\begin{array}{cccc}
 & \bullet & & \\
 & \bullet & \bullet & \\
\bullet & \bullet & \bullet & \\
\bullet & \bullet & \bullet & \bullet
\end{array}
$$

Having displayed a number in that manner, the Pythagoreans very naturally thought of it as a spatial object, especially when objections to so thinking had not yet been worked out. The number 1, which would be represented by a single pebble, dot, or whatever, has a very special place in this scheme: repeated applications of the number 1, repeated use of single pebbles, generates the number series. Second, the notational system employed encouraged the Pythagoreans to think of the number 1 not only as the arithmetical unit but also as the unit of geometry, namely as the *point*. In this system, the number 1 appears as a single dot, a single point, and from such points geometrical figures can be generated, as with the triangular number 10. But that is exactly what geometers say: from points come lines, from lines planes, from planes come geometrical solids. There is yet more: this combined arithmetical-geometrical unit came to seem to the Pythagoreans to be also the *ultimate physical unit*. Repeated applications of one and the same unit (say pebbles) can generate further numbers (say the number 10), and geometrical figures (a triangle), and also a genuine *physical object* (a triangle constructed out of rocks). Once the arithmetical unit comes to be thought of as a unit piece of matter, we can see why the Pythagorean mathematization of the world included the belief that things are numbers.

The Discovery of Incommensurability
It is misleading to say that the Pythagoreans thought of natural phenomena as expressions of number and leave it at that. What needs to be mentioned is what they recognized as numbers. The mathematics of that period included as numbers what we today would call the "natural numbers" (1, 2, 3 . . .) and fractions ($1/2$, $2/7$), which were thought of as ratios of natural numbers. Hence, when the Pythagoreans held that accounts of the world and its order would be numerical, that things are (made of) numbers, they had in mind that the numbers would be natural numbers, whether as whole numbers or as ratios of them. That belief was shattered by a mathematical discovery made by a Greek mathematician, perhaps a Pythagorean, about 450 B.C.E.

The Pythagorean theorem says that the square of the hypotenuse of a right triangle is equal to the sum of the squares of the two remaining sides. The Pythagorean view of the universe encounters no difficulty if the two sides are, say, 4 and 3 units: because $4^2 + 3^2 = 25$ and the square root of 25 is 5. Thus the lengths of all three sides can be expressed as natural numbers and so the relationships of the sides can be compared in terms of natural numbers; for example, "this side is $4/5$ of the length of the hypotenuse." Imagine, however, a right triangle in which the sides that form the right angle have a length of 1 (unit) each. Then $1^2 + 1^2 = 2$. The square root of 2 will be the length of the hypotenuse. But the square root of 2 cannot be expressed as a natural number, and hence the ratio of that side to the hypotenuse is $1/. . . .$ The hypotenuse is *incommensurable* with the other sides; no common basis of comparison exists.

Here was a piece of reality not comprehendable within the number system (as then understood). The shock to the Pythagoreans must have been great, because the discovery established what seemed to be irrationality in the universe. (Notice that we still speak of numbers such as the square root of 2 as *irrationals*.) Until mathematicians could see their way to thinking of such things as "the square root of 2" as a new type of number, the Pythagorean idea that the world is numerically intelligible, and thus a model for spiritual emulation, was falsified.

The Ultimate Principles: Limit and the Unlimited

Although number was the Pythagoreans' principle of *objects*, they did not consider number the ultimate constituent of the universe. Numbers themselves have principles, and those are referred to in the most general description of the world.

We can produce a triangle (say) on an otherwise undisturbed expanse of sand (or paper) by drawing some lines. Those lines make a figure, an object, in the previously unordered sand by delimiting a certain area. The triangle is just that shape produced by limiting a certain area through the act of introducing boundaries. A similar lesson about the creation of order was equally suggested by Pythagoras' musical discovery.

> The [scale], moreover, is limited, both externally by the octave (for the scale ends, as we say, "on the same note" and begins again in endless recurrence), and internally. . . . The introduction of this system marks out the whole unlimited field of sound, which ranges indefinitely in opposite directions (high and low). The infinite variety of quality in sound is reduced to order by the exact and simple law of ratio in quantity. The system so defined still contains the unlimited in the blank intervals between the notes; but the unlimited is no longer an orderless continuum; it is confined within an order, a *kosmos*, by the imposition of Limit or Measure. (Cornford, 1974, pp. 143–144)

From such reflections came the Pythagoreans' two ultimate principles: *limit* and *the unlimited*. (It should be remembered that the *apeiron*, the unlimited, was Anaximander's basic stuff, the *arché* of the universe for him.) Any system of order, including the universe as a whole, is the consequence of introducing limits into an otherwise formless chaos and thereby producing something limited, that is, existing things.

Thus, in Pythagorean thought we find two ultimate principles involved in the creation of a world. Such a view is called *dualistic* in contrast with the various monistic systems of Pythagoras' predecessors.

The Opposites

The Pythagoreans took over and extended the idea that the world is characterized by opposites and opposition (conflict). It turns out that, for them, the *primary* opposition of *limit* and *unlimited* manifests itself in a variety of different contexts under different names.

Very closely associated with the primary pair of opposites were *odd* and *even*, which are best understood as the numerical aspects of limited and unlimited. A more extended listing and linking of aspects of the ultimate principles appears in some Pythagorean accounts:

limit	unlimited
odd	even
one	plurality
right	left
male	female
at rest	moving
straight	crooked
light	darkness
good	bad
square	oblong

That list, including as it does "good" and "bad," reveals that the two principles are *moral* as well as *descriptive* features of the universe. (Notice which items are lumped with *good* and which with *bad*—an important social comment is embodied in the placement of male and female in this schema of conflict.) Limit is the principle of goodness; the unlimited, the principle of evil. Pythagoreans, however, seem less apt to regard the universe as a perpetual battleground between warring principles than did Anaximander (or the earlier Persian religious leader Zoroaster, with whom the Greeks sometimes linked Pythagoras). Order, beauty, and harmony are achieved when members of the first list establish dominance over their counterparts on the second list. Pythagoreans tended to think that there are extensive regions of the world in which permanent dominance of harmony over chaos has been achieved (the heavenly bodies, the system of musical sound) or else can be achieved (here the individual *psyché* is the important example).

Pythagorean Cosmogony and Cosmology

Limit and the unlimited, in their numerical guise as the odd and the even, give rise to the first created object, the *Unit* (the One, the Monad). That Unit is, of course, nothing other than the number 1, thought of in the Pythagorean manner as an object. It is possible that the creation of the num-

ber 1 was thought of biologically as the insertion of a seed by the male principle of limit into the unlimited, which was conceived of as a female.

> Apparently the first unit, like other living things, began at once to
> grow, and somehow as the result of growth burst asunder into two;
> whereupon the void, fulfilling its proper function, keeps the two units
> apart, and thus, owing to the confusion of the units of arithmetic with
> the points of geometry, brings into existence not only the number 2 but
> also the line. So the process is begun which, continuing indefinitely, is to
> result in the visible universe as we know it. (Kirk and Raven, 1960, p. 253)

The Unit, the first number, generates the number series. But the generation of numbers is simultaneously the generation of geometrical figures
and also the production of physical objects. Various Pythagoreans seem to
have conceived the details of this process in different ways.

Two items of Pythagorean cosmology are of interest here, not only
because of their historical significance but also because they show how the
different features of Pythagorean thinking were woven together. One item is
the famous Pythagorean doctrine of the *harmony of the spheres.*

Bodies whirring around—say, a piece of wood on a string—produce a
sound; hence the planets and the stars must also do so (it was said). The
faster the piece of wood moves, the more highly pitched the sound; so too
must that be true of the heavenly bodies. As the bodies furthest away from
the center must move correspondingly faster to keep pace with the more
interior planets, pitch will progressively rise as one proceeds from the interior heavenly bodies to the stars. To that line of reasoning was now applied
the numerical discovery concerning the musical scales. The sun, stars, Mars,
and so on are not equally distant from each other. Instead, their relative distances vary in ratios corresponding to the distance between the notes of a
musical scale. Hence, the constant sounds they produce must be (!) harmo-
nious, concordant. But why do we not *hear* those "touches of sweet harmony"
(as Shakespeare referred to them in *The Merchant of Venice,* Act 5, Scene 1)?
The answer is, incarnation is a punishment, and not being able to hear "the
music of the spheres" is part of our punishment.

Equally famous as a Pythagorean doctrine—although created by the
important Pythagorean Philolaus *(Phil-o-lawus')* sometime in the mid to late
fifth century—was a new planetary theory. The chief feature of this strikingly
different conception of the structure of the heavens is that the earth was
considered to *move.* Hitherto, in both ordinary belief and astronomical theory, the earth had been located at the center of the universe, with the other
astronomical bodies circling around it. The earth, previously thought of as
flat on top, was now said to be spherical, and was removed from the center of
the world and made to be a planet, to circle around the center. The theory
was not heliocentric, for the sun was still counted a planet. Instead, the theory held—most probably because of a religious belief in the importance of

fire—that the center of the universe was occupied by the Central Fire. Around that circled the earth, moon, sun, the five known planets, and the stars. Yet, in characteristic Pythagorean fashion, that could not be the complete story. On that count, the heavenly bodies add up only to nine. Ten, however, is the sacred number. Hence, an additional (tenth) body must be moving around the Central Fire. So was inferred the existence of the Counterearth, another planet that, like the Central Fire, cannot be seen from the earth because we inhabit the wrong side of the planet.

Pythagorean Reflections on Social Order

An account of Pythagorean philosophy should mention what it had to say about the political order, even though its political theory was developed only in a most elementary manner compared with the remainder of the system. Those ideas about political life were probably a quite early constituent of Pythagorean thought. Pythagoras, after all, had founded an organized sect and that had quickly become a political force in the city-states of southern Italy. Thus, considerations operating from the beginning of Pythagoreanism would ensure that some thought be given to how to live properly within a human community.

The central principles of that social theory are an extension of Pythagoras' basic teaching about the human *psyché* and the cosmos. An individual can be brought to mirror the great cosmos. That is the fundamental aim of Pythagorean religious life. So, too, the communal life of human beings will be properly organized when it exhibits the same principles of harmony applicable both to the *psyché* and to the cosmos. Those patterns of order are produced by imposing boundaries on the chaotic raw material of social life, by introducing limits into the social unlimited:

> The doctrine of harmony is meant to apply to the social order as well. This order too is made of diverse elements: good and bad, well-born and base-born, rich and poor. If the social order is to reflect the nature of the world-order as a whole, these diverse elements must be bound together in harmony and friendship. (Robinson, 1968, p. 80)

If a society is to achieve a genuine harmony, two conditions pertaining to those pairs of social opposites must be fulfilled: (1) the good member of each pair must establish dominance over the evil member, and (2) the subordinate opposite must acquiesce. (Plato made these principles central in the social arrangements of the *Republic*, with the exception that "male" and "female" were implicitly removed from the list of opposites and the propriety of male dominance explicitly denied.)

In pushing its social theory beyond that account of harmony, Pythagoreanism was not so fortunate. Given their predilection for mathematics, it is to be expected that Pythagoreans attempted to treat the political realm quantitatively. The traditional Greek maxim, which was very appropriate to Pythagorean ideas of social harmony, "Give everyone his due," looked as if it might have a mathematical interpretation of "due." Their enthusiasm led them on. If it is true that *all* things are number, then why not justice, marriage, and so on? Those notions, which are central to an account of social life, were treated mathematically by the Pythagoreans, but not in any way helpful to political theory. They not only claimed that justice, for example, was a number, but they also said it was the number 4. That kind of account of human virtues and institutions led nowhere.

PYTHAGOREAN INFLUENCE

Pythagoras and his followers must be credited with a striking intellectual accomplishment. They succeeded in producing a set of ideas that are not only important and interesting in themselves but are also expressions of one major type of intellectual temperament. Thus, having marked out a certain passionate and religious style of thinking, Pythagoreanism did not vanish with the passing of the sect the master had founded, but instead continued to attract adherents down through the centuries.

Plato played the leading role in the transmission of Pythagorean thought. He was in many respects the very model of a Pythagorean mind and temperament. With his enormous intellectual and artistic powers, he was able to take Pythagorean themes and to refashion, extend, and defend them with exceptional skill. Later Pythagorean thought was shaped as much by Plato as by the earlier stages of the movement.

Various Pythagorean revivals have occurred in the history of Western thought. Probably the most important outbreak was in the sixteenth century, when a surge of interest in Pythagorean ideas was a central factor in those changes in astronomy and mechanics that ushered in the Scientific Revolution and modern science. Copernicus found in Pythagorean cosmology justification for putting the sun at the center of the world and for making the earth move around it. Kepler's consuming search for mathematical harmonies in the heavens—a search rewarded on three occasions—was pure Pythagoreanism. Lastly, Galileo, who was Ionian and not Pythagorean in spirit, nonetheless perfectly expressed the mathematizing ideal of Pythagorean philosophy:

> Philosophy is written in the great book which is ever before our eyes—I mean the universe—but we cannot understand it if we do not first learn the language and grasp the symbols in which it is written. The book is written in the mathematical language, and the symbols are triangles, circles, and other geometrical figures, without whose help it is impossible to comprehend a single word of it; without which one wanders in vain through a dark labyrinth. (Galileo, quoted in E. A. Burtt, *The Metaphysical Foundations of Modern Science*, rev. ed. [Garden City, N.Y.: Doubleday, 1954], p. 75)

Again, Einstein's claim that a cosmic religious feeling is the best and strongest motive for scientific research is an expression of the Pythagorean attitude that has lived on into twentieth-century science.

BIBLIOGRAPHY

W. K. C. Guthrie, *The Greeks and Their Gods* (Boston: Beacon Press, 1950).
  See Chapter 11 on the Orphics. Or see Guthries's article "Orphism" in Paul Edwards, ed., Encyclopedia of Philosophy (New York: Macmillan, 1967).
F. M. Cornford, "Mysticism and Science in the Pythagorean Tradition," reprinted in A. P. D. Mourelatos, ed., *The Pre-Socratics* (Garden City, N.Y.: Anchor Books, 1974). Originally published in *Classical Quarterly* 16 (1922) and 17 (1923).
  Although much of this essay is rejected by contemporary scholars, pages 137–139 are relevant to the socioreligious background of Pythagoreanism.
Charles H. Kahn, "Pythagorean Philosophy Before Plato," in A. P. D. Mourelatos, ed., *The Pre-Socratics* (Garden City, N.Y.: Anchor Books, 1974).
  A very good view of the state of studies on Pythagoras.
Arthur Koestler, *The Sleepwalkers* (New York: Macmillan, 1959).
  A very readable account of the creation of modern heliocentric planetary theory that emphasizes the Pythagorean contribution (and that was written by a contemporary Pythagorean enthusiast).

6

HERACLITUS

Since we possess over a hundred genuine fragments of his writing, it might seem that no serious problems could arise concerning the interpretation of Heraclitus *(Hera-cli'-tus)*. But that is far from the truth. Every student approaching Heraclitus for the first time should realize that views about what he *meant* are more subject to revision than is the case for other Pre-Socratics. It is most unlikely that the final story about Heraclitus has yet been told—and even if it has, scholars have not yet been able to determine just which story is that last word.

One chief difficulty in interpreting Heraclitus is a consequence of his writing style. The ancient world called him the Riddler, the Obscure, and seems not to have understood him well. Although he did write in prose—the new language of Ionian inquiry—his prose was not prosaic, was not standard "reporting" prose. Rather, he expressed himself in aphorisms—short, pungent sayings. Even worse, those terse remarks were not straightforward pieces of wisdom such as the traditional "Know thyself." They were instead filled with verbal play, with ambiguity, were intentionally puzzling, paradoxical, even riddling. Think of a book consisting of virtually nothing but enigmatic remarks such as "Though they hear they are like the deaf. The saying describes them: present yet absent"; and "Men do not know how to hear or to speak"; "I searched for myself"; "Aion [Life? Time?] is a child playing checkers. The child is king." Obviously, although many fragments exist, we must ask what each means and must struggle to find an answer.

Those difficulties in understanding Heraclitus that are caused by his style have been compounded by an interpretative framework that misdiagnoses his philosophical intentions. Since Aristotle, Heraclitus has typically been regarded as the next in the succession of Ionian cosmologists, a *physicist* whose aim was to develop the same kind of theory as Anaximander or Anaximenes, but who believed that fire, not water or air, is the chief stuff of the world. In that view, his style was seen as an incidental idiosyncrasy, to be explained by a pathological mental condition or (more plausibly) by his contemptuous desire to make it very difficult for stupid humanity to understand him.

The long-term trend in interpreting Heraclitus has been away from that view, away from the idea that he was a cosmologist who happened to have a strange way of expressing himself. Instead, interpreters have increasingly tended to see him as someone who reflected on, borrowed from, and worked out some implications of the new scientific movement, but whose chief intellectual aims and contributions were not cosmological. Moreover, the idea is now widely accepted that his style is an integral, not incidental, part of his aims in writing and is intimately connected with his vision of human life and the world in which it is lived.

Heraclitus was a native and lifelong resident of the important Ionian *polis* of Ephesus *(Eff'-ess-us)*. The geography of philosophy was still quite confined (as to be expected of a small culture growing slowly). Ephesus was twenty-five miles up the coast from Miletus, just past Pythagoras' home island of Samos and only a short distance south of Xenophanes' Colophon. His dates are approximate: 540–480 B.C.E. That places his birth immediately after the Greek city-states in Asia Minor fell under Persian rule. Their revolt against that domination in 499 B.C.E. was led by Miletus, and with the reassertion of Persian rule, Miletus was destroyed by the victors. Ephesus then became, and long remained, the leading Greek community in Ionia. Heraclitus' death roughly coincided with the great Greek victories over the Persians in 490 and again in 480 B.C.E.

He seems to have been the eldest son of the royal family of the city; it is said that he declined the kingship when it fell to him. The fragments make it clear that he had considerable distaste for his fellow human beings, including his fellow townspeople. Fragment 121 says, "All the grown men in Ephesus ought to hang themselves and leave the city to the boys. . . . ." That intense dislike of, and contempt for, others kept him from having personal associates and disciples. Whatever influence he had—and that included possibly Parmenides and certainly Plato—was exercised entirely through his writing.

The fragments of his book we possess probably constitute a significant portion of the original. We do not know, however, in what order the various sayings we have were arranged, although in all likelihood they were intelligibly organized rather than being a random collection of thoughts.

THE DEBATE OVER WISDOM

Heraclitus' aims are best grasped when he is seen as a participant in the early phase of a cultural debate over what was to count as wisdom and hence over who should be thought of as *wise*.

The poets had functioned as the repositories of the culture's knowledge (historical, religious, political, moral, cosmological, and even technical) and so were reckoned to be *sophos*, wise. In the early sixth century B.C.E., another group, loosely related to the poets, came to the force: the Sages, whose wisdom was largely political and was expressed in *proverbs*. In addition, the small but confident new intellectual movement from Ionia had begun to issue challenges to the authority of those dominant figures. Whether or not Pythagoras was the first to call himself *philosophos*, "lover of wisdom," the story that maintained that he was the first does reflect the fact that practitioners of the new modes of inquiry were beginning to claim the culture's intellectual leadership.

Heraclitus condemned the three chief representatives of the poetic tradition, Homer, Hesiod, and Archilochus *(Ar-kill'-o-cuss)*, and so, by implication, he rejected the entire tradition's claim to wisdom: "Most men learn from Hesiod, who is taken to know the most. Yet he could not tell day and night . . ." and "Homer and Archilochus deserve to be kicked out of the competition and given beatings" (Fragments 57 and 42). Although Heraclitus does wish to assimilate the outlook of the new thinkers, nonetheless the publicly known figures of *historie* are subjected to strong criticism: "Much learning does not produce understanding. Otherwise it would have taught Hesiod and Pythagoras, and also Xenophanes and Hecataeus" (Fragment 40; Hecataeus *[Heck-at-ae-us']* was a Milesian who specialized in the geographical and cross-cultural branches of inquiry.)

While largely silent about the Sages, Heraclitus' own practice of writing in aphorisms, rather than in meter or in discursive prose, was probably an attempt on his part to claim that he was the inheritor of that line of wisdom. Even more certainly, both the aphoristic style and the other obvious feature of his style—the enigmatic and ambiguous nature of his pronouncements—were intended to claim that he was related to another famous source of wisdom, this time a supernatural one. The oracle at Delphi gave Apollo's answer, spoken through the mouth of a priestess, to questions put to it. Those answers typically had double meanings and required interpretation, although the questioner did not always have the sense to realize that. Heraclitus' style was designed to be like Apollo's: "The lord whose oracle is at Delphi neither states nor hides but gives a sign" (Fragment 93). So too Heraclitus, and the universe itself, as we shall see later, neither states nor conceals, but gives *signs* of the truth. It requires intelligence to work out the truth, to infer it from the signs presented to the senses, whether those signs are produced by nature or by Heraclitus.

IGNORANCE AND THE HUMAN CONDITION

Heraclitus sought to point the way to the truth about the way things are, a truth not grasped by any of the traditional sages or by the recent challengers to the title. His own claim to have succeeded rested on a distinction between *knowledge* and *wisdom*. Pythagoras, for instance, knew a great deal but lacked what wisdom requires: an understanding of the *meaning* of all those things he knew. The *insight* is precisely what Heraclitus considered he himself has achieved.

The results of inquiry are superior to a poet's quite conventional accounts of the world: "What we see, hear, experience: that I prefer most" (Fragment 55). On those grounds, Heraclitus was willing to be affiliated with the new intellectual movement in opposition to the authority of the poets. Yet research also has its limits: "Eyes and ears make bad witnesses if men cannot understand what they say" (Fragment 107).

For Heraclitus, that inability to understand what our senses tell us, an inability to read the signs thrown up by the world, is the common lot of human beings, whether they be specialized inquirers or ordinary people. He was wholly pessimistic about the ability of people to grasp the truth even when they heard it stated. The opening words of the book express that pessimism: "Though this *logos* is always so, men never understand it, neither before nor after they have heard it. For although all things happen in accordance with this *logos*, it is as if other men had no experience of it when they meet those words and acts which I set forth, distinguishing each according to its nature and saying how it is. But then other men do not understand their own waking acts, just as they forget what they do in sleep" (Fragment 1).

LOGOS

Those first words of the book also introduce the central notion of Heraclitus' account of the world, the *logos*. It is impossible to give a simple account of what the *logos* was thought to be, although translators and commentators will (inevitably) attempt to provide a formula. The word *logos* was very common in Greek usage, with a large number of different though related meanings. (It is also the source of many English words; for example, "logical," "biology," and the presently popular "logo.") Kahn gives the following definitions of the word *logos:* saying, speech, discourse, statement, report; account, explanation, reason, principle; esteem, reputation; collection, enumeration, ratio, proportion." (See the Bibliography at the end of the chapter for Kahn, 1979. The quote is from p. 29, footnote. For an even more extensive, and not identical, account of the meaning of *logos,* see Guthrie, 1962, Vol. 1, pp. 420–424.)

The word *logos* came from a verb meaning "to speak" and at the simplest level meant "word." But it can also mean "what is said," where what is said is not identical with the words used to say it (what two people say can be the same even though they say it in different languages, using different words). Branching off from that idea is the notion of being well-spoken: *logos* can mean something like "rational discourse." From there it is a short step to mean that which makes discourse rational, namely the reasons, arguments, accounts embedded in the talk. And so on.

All those meanings of the ordinary term, and more, are involved in Heraclitus' use of the word *logos* to mark off his central theoretical conception.

Fragment 2 contains the statement "the *logos* is common to all." Probably the least misleading short explanation of what Heraclitus took the *logos* to be is that he thought of it as a *rationality* that is shared by all things. Yet even that account is ambiguous. It might mean, and Heraclitus did mean, that all things exemplify a rational pattern. Here he would be emphasizing, with his predecessors, that the basic fact about the world is that it is intelligibly organized. Nonetheless, in saying that the *logos* is common to everything, Heraclitus probably meant more than that. All things are also rational in that they are intelligent. Things are not only part of some rational, intelligent system, but they are also, in some way, rational, intelligent *beings*. "Thinking is common to all" (Fragment 113). For Heraclitus, the outcome of thought is to be found everywhere in the world, but then so too is thought itself.

We have already seen that Heraclitus acknowledges two different types of rationality: (1) the knowledge of (many) things and (2) the wisdom that has insight into those various facts. Clearly, the *logos* that runs through everything is connected with wisdom, with the understanding or comprehension of what is fundamental to the activities of the universe.

The *logos*, both as active wisdom and as the outcome of exercising that capacity, runs the world. Heraclitus borrows Anaximander's image of the helmsman piloting the ship of the world: ". . . all things come to be in accordance with the *logos* . . ." and "Wisdom is one, knowing the thought by which it steers all things through all things" (Fragments 1 and 41).

It should be obvious that the *logos* will also turn out to be the chief divinity in the Heraclitean world: the built-in wisdom through which the events of the world are organized.

A LINGUISTIC WORLD

For Heraclitus, human wisdom consists in grasping the *logos*, in the apprehension of cosmic wisdom. Although the discoveries of Milesian science help reveal new aspects of the *logos*, Heraclitus thought that the possibility of achieving understanding is open to all people. One need not become a practitioner of inquiry, as Pythagoras thought, to acquire the appropriate insight into the ways of the world. Nevertheless, the vast majority of people will not become wise, will not grasp the *logos*. Heraclitus represents that failure as being of the same kind as an inability to understand what is said in a language.

That linguistic explanation of human ignorance is intimately tied to his view that the rationality of the universe is embodied in what he calls the *logos*. As we have seen, the word *logos* had its roots in talk about language, meaning basically "words" or "what is said." Since he thinks that the central feature of the world is the existence of a *logos*, it follows that he conceives of the world as a highly complex language. That world speaks to us, if we can but understand. It consists of *signs,* if we can read them right, if we can learn how to decipher them. The Pythagoreans offered mathematics as the key to understanding—Heraclitus offers *language.* God is not a geometer, but is rather the author of wise discourse, a system of meaning.

One of Heraclitus' chief philosophical contributions is to have first suggested that linguistic model, or picture of the world, as a language. In the course of Western thought since Heraclitus, that model has surfaced many times, competing with other such broad pictures (the world thought of as an organism or as a machine) as representations of the nature of nature.

OUR MISCONCEPTIONS: VARIETY, INDEPENDENCE, STABILITY, AND CONCORD

What must we understand to be wise? What are the fundamental principles of cosmic wisdom and rationality?

Several interconnected ideas constitute Heraclitean wisdom. Before I discuss some of them, it is important to realize that for Heraclitus the deplorable condition of human understanding does not consist in its being a void, does not consist in a simple *lack* of knowledge. Instead, we suffer from a number of fundamental *mis*conceptions about what the world is like and how it operates. We think we comprehend the world, but we do not. Hence the message of the *logos* is contrary to our beliefs. The first step on the road to wisdom must be to identify our misconceptions (a thesis that Socrates also held).

Taking "world" very broadly to include what is social and natural, personal and public, human and divine, we humans think that the world is composed of a number of *different* things, states, conditions, and so forth. These various items that constitute the objects of our experience are largely and significantly *independent* of each other. They do change, of course, yet they are fundamentally *stable.* And they manage to coexist in a state of relative concord, *harmony.* Heraclitus was out to challenge those ways of thinking in the name of the *logos.*

Or so *I* say. At this point the interpretation of Heraclitus becomes very unsettled. In making his discussion of human understanding central, as I am doing, I am presenting Heraclitus as much more like a modern philosopher than is usually done.

CHANGE, THE RIVER, AND IDENTITY

One of Heraclitus' major themes concerns the extent and role of change in the world. What is called "the Heraclitean doctrine of flux" is his claim that *all* things are *always* changing. Although some people have recently denied that Heraclitus had such a view, the ancient world regarded that insistence on universal change as *the* characteristic doctrine of Heraclitus. Plato was deeply influenced by it and made flux central to his own account of the material world.

Heraclitus certainly did not think that he was teaching humanity that all things are *subject* to change, though he may well have thought that we need reminders of that. He may have thought it is news to most people that all things are always, at every moment, changing. Those changes are continually taking place, although *typically* we do not, at the time, observe them. Most often, changes (say in a friend's appearance) become noticeable only after many small imperceptible changes have produced a cumulative impact. Heraclitus thought we must *infer* the constancy of change from such facts.

Yet continual change is not at the center of Heraclitus' vision of a changing universe. Plato took the doctrine of flux to have a *moral:* that we cannot have any knowledge about material things because they are always changing. Heraclitus too would have been less interested in the claimed ubiquity of change than in its significance for human thought and life. What lesson should a wise person learn from recognizing the centrality of change in the world?

My guess is that the appropriate insight is something like the following: Although we humans are aware that all things change, although we may be intelligent enough to infer that things are always changing, nonetheless we persist in regarding change as a deviation from the norm, as something that requires explanation. We wonder why there is a nick in the fender today, why the wind began to blow, why people's hair gets thinner as they age, why you don't love me like you used to do. All those worries are a result of misconceiving the status of change, according to Heraclitus. Change is the *normal* state of affairs. A wise man is not surprised that his possessions wear out, that people no longer look the same, or that their thoughts, feelings, and intentions are inconsistent. Rather, wisdom would consist in being struck by the elements of *stability* in the world, by the continuities that exist despite changes. The sun rises at different times and places on the horizon, but what we should wonder at, and attempt to explain, is why it always rises in the east. Why does she still love me? How is it to be explained that my coat remains basically blue for quite some time? And so on.

No doubt exists that Heraclitus said *something* about a river, that he used the idea of a river with its constantly flowing waters as a symbol of the perpetual changes found in everything. Precisely what he said is in doubt, however. And the implications of the two alternatives are wholly different. Many would insist that the correct quote is "Upon those who step into the same rivers, different and again different waters flow" (Fragment 12). Here it is possible for someone to step twice into the same river and the point of the quote would be a quasi-Pythagorean thought that the material constituent of a thing is not what makes it the same thing despite having undergone changes. Yet since antiquity, the most famous saying of Heraclitus has been the *other* version: "You cannot step into the same river twice," which probably continued "for different and again different waters flow" (Fragment 91). That version implies a different thesis: despite our thought and talk that it is the *same* river flowing past us from moment to moment, it is not, strictly, one and the same river at all, for it has changed, it is different and so not the same.

Many scholars think it implausible that Heraclitus held such a strong thesis; nonetheless, that latter view is compatible with his attempts to alter our ordinary ways of thinking about change. Of all human misconceptions about change, Heraclitus would think that the deepest misconception is the belief that *things* change. The sage, in his eyes, would recognize that *things* do not change; rather, change calls things into being. And since Heraclitus held that change constantly occurs, it follows that nothing is the same object from moment to moment.

As previously mentioned, little in the earliest Pre-Socratics would be appropriately arguable by modern philosophers. However, the problems of *identity* raised by Heraclitus' river image are still a staple of philosophical discussion. In that regard, Heraclitus has a claim to being the first philosopher (or perhaps the first metaphysician).

Even though we should talk of change producing a succession of new entities rather than thinking that change modifies continuing objects, Heraclitus would also insist that we should be struck by *how much alike* any two successor objects are. Despite what is in one way radical change, we must be astonished by the continuities and seek to explain them. Imagine living in a world where changes consisted of random and total alterations in the appearance and behavior of things. That changes in our world are not random is a sign of the functioning of the *logos*. One meaning of *logos* was "ratio" or "proportion." A part of the rationality of the world, its wise guidance by the *logos*, consists in changes being (on the whole) orderly, regular, measured, instead of chaotic, unintelligible. As in Anaximander, change operates in a lawful manner.

UNITY

Our conception of the world, according to Heraclitus, includes more than the idea of its being populated by objects that undergo change. We think that the furniture of the world is made up of many many such things of numerous different kinds. Furthermore, we think the objects that constitute the world are independent existences: a pair of sandals in Miletus, a rain shower in Crete, a flea in Sparta, all seem to us to come and go without reference to each other.

Heraclitus thinks that entire suite of conceptions misguided. In Fragment 50, after first reminding us that he is but the mouthpiece through which cosmic wisdom speaks, he states what the sage knows to be the truth about these matters: "Listening not to me but to the Logos, it is wise to agree that all things are one." Behind the apparent diversity of the world is unity. *All things are one.*

One chief source for that claim is obvious. Anaximenes, for instance, had held that all things in the universe are but transformations of *one* original kind of stuff. Heraclitus adopts that cosmological notion and uses it to deny that the world is not, as we think, made up of many entities that are both different and independent.

The doctrine of unity was intended to do more than bind horses, spoons, and stars into one system of matter. In fact, the most difficult and the most important part of presenting the world as a unity remains to be accomplished.

An objector might say that "All things are one" may work for horses and so on because Heraclitus can show a unity in such things by using the idea that there is only a single stuff that manifests itself in a large number of temporary clumps that we think of as individual objects. However, what about other features of the world—such things as day and night, for instance? The world comprises *opposites* as well as horses and spoons (which are different, but not opposed). Things that stand in opposition to each other, the objection concludes, cannot be said to be *one,* to be a unity.

On the contrary, one of Heraclitus' chief contentions is that opposites are really the same, that the doctrine of unity also extends to pairs of opposites. For instance, Fragment 57, which has already been partially quoted, says in full "Most men learn from Hesiod, who is taken to know the most. Yet he could not tell day and night: for they are one."

He did not mean by asserting the sameness of opposites that *no* difference exists between them—between day and night or between sleeping and waking, for example. The unity of horses and spoons was asserted without denying the differences between them. Rather, just as horses and spoons are bound together in some nonobvious underlying system (in fact, a system of material transformations), so too are those things, states, and conditions that are joined in opposition. Some *logos* connects each pair, some rational explanation that shows the opposing items to be a unity. The *logos,* the account, of what produces the hidden unity will not be the same for different pairs of opposites. That fact can be illustrated by examining some of the cases in which Heraclitus holds that two opposites are the same and by noticing what the implied rationale for the claim of unity would be:

1. "Disease makes health pleasant and good, hunger fullness, weariness rest" (Fragment 111). Here the secret connection is that the negative member of each pair is precisely what produces the desirability of the positive state. We enjoy rest and find it good only because of its contrast with weariness. In that way, each of those pairs is a unity.

2. "The way up and the way back are the same" (Fragment 60). The road one takes to get somewhere is also the way home. Here the same object functions as both members of an opposition.

3. "The way of the pen (?) is both straight and crooked" (Fragment 59). The pen's movement is both straight (across the page) and crooked (as it forms the letters). The opposition "straight" and "crooked" contains items that are connected as different aspects of the behavior of an object.

4. Day and night are not to be thought of as separate cosmological powers, as Hesiod did. They are different portions of a single day, portions produced by the presence or absence of sun.

5. "Sea water is the most pure and the most polluted: it is drinkable and life-sustaining for fish, undrinkable and deadly for men" (Fragment 61). Here the opposed conditions of purity and pollution can be true of the same object, depending on what kind of being is making the assessment.

We have not yet completed the account of how all things are one. Heraclitus first tells us that (in a twentieth-century phrase) dualisms are untenable. That is, all opposed pairs will be found, on inquiry, to be really a unity, bound together by some *logos* or the other (those various *logoi* themselves being only different manifestations of the *logos*).

He then goes one step further: all those structures that are units composed of opposites rationally connected are themselves only different aspects of a single whole. Here the key fragment is the first sentence of Fragment 67: "God: day and night, winter and summer, war and peace, fullness and hunger." An ancient commentator noted at this point that Heraclitus meant *all* the opposites. Every pair is thus connected with every other pair as a different aspect of the whole system that is here referred to as "God" (of which more later).

THE ONE AND THE MANY

"All things are one." This thesis is, and was intended to be, paradoxical. How can there be many things that are nonetheless one thing? Heraclitus bequeathed not only his answer but also a certain way of conceptualizing the problem: what is the relation between the one and the many? The Greeks went on to employ that formula to describe the structure of their most significant philosophical problems. Not only were questions about the relation of individual things to an underlying matter conceived of as issues concerning the relation of the one and the many, but so too were problems about the relation between individuals and the state and, with Socrates, problems about the relation between instances of a concept (individual dogs, say) and the concept itself (what it is to be a dog). The conception of philosophical problems as arising from trying to understand the relation between (1) many somethings and (2) one something else became common in later Greek philosophy.

PEACE

There is one other fundamental conception of "common sense" that Heraclitus opposed, in the name of wisdom. People (according to Heraclitus) believe that the world's normal condition is one of peaceful coexistence among the component things of that world. Strife, conflict, competition, violence, and war are regarded as out of the ordinary. The occurrence of those conditions requires explanation. We ask, "Why must he be so competitive?" and "Why did war break out?" We don't (normally) ask, "Why haven't you hit anyone today?" or "Why did peace break out?"

Of course, the world is filled with strife and striving. Human beings, however, think that there *should* be concord; they dream of a world where the norm of peaceful coexistence is fully realized. We would like to see the day when the lion lies down with the lamb.

Pythagoras and his followers made harmony a central feature of their description of the world. Their idea of what harmony or proper attunement consists in was a version of that ordinary picture of peace and reconciliation. They took harmony to be teamwork, "one for all and all for one," each willingly performing his or her own part, whatever it happened to be.

Heraclitus would have none of that.

WAR

One might think that, because of his stress on the unity of opposites, Heraclitus would be attracted to the picture of a world in which objects peacefully coexisted. He did not, however, hold that opposites do not stand in opposition. What he denied was only that each member of a pair of opposites is an independent constituent of the world. The unity of a pair consists in some underlying rational connection between them, a connection that produces an intelligible system of opposition, not the absence of opposition. All such pairs are further joined into one interconnected system, called "the world" or "nature" (or "God").

Heraclitus adopts and extends Anaximander's scheme whereby the world is marked by change and where change is characterized as a process involving strife, encroachment, destruction. He holds that all things are always changing, although at the time the changes are most often imperceptible. Now, in a precisely similar fashion, he holds that conflict is *always* present (since change is conflict), even though, most of the time, that conflict is not perceptible.

Fragment 51 is a major presentation of the doctrine of permanent conflict. Unfortunately, that fragment is subject to a variety of sensible readings. Hence what follows is a loose translation. "[People] do not understand how a thing can be in agreement by differing: harmony is opposing tensions, as in the bow and the lyre." Not only is the wording of the saying in doubt, so too is the proper interpretation of the central image of the bow and lyre. The following passage from Guthrie probably cannot be improved on:

> Everywhere there are forces pulling both ways at once. *Apparent* harmony, rest, or peace is in the real constitution of things *(physis)* a state of precarious equilibrium between these forces. Look at a strung bow lying on the ground or leaning against a wall. No movement is visible. To the eyes it appears a static object, completely at rest. But in fact a continuous tug-of-war is going on within it, as will become evident if the string is not strong enough, or is allowed to perish. The bow will immediately take advantage, snap it and leap to straighten itself, thus showing that each had been putting forth effort all the time. The *harmonia* was a dynamic one of vigorous and contrary motions neutralized by equilibrium and so unapparent. The state of a tuned lyre (or for that matter violin) is similar, as any player whose string has broken knows to his chagrin. And the point is that the functioning of both instruments, their very nature as a working bow or lyre, is dependent on this balance of forces, which is therefore *good*. . . . For Heraclitus bow and lyre symbolize the whole cosmos, which without such constant "warfare" would disintegrate and perish. Well may he say ([Fragment] 54): Invisible *harmonia* is stronger than (or superior to) visible." As far as visible connexion goes, the bow might be naturally bent and the string simply tied to it at either end; the invisible connexion between them is the element of struggle, of dynamic opposition. So it is that "Nature loves concealment" ([Fragment] 123). (Guthrie, 1962, Vol. 1, pp. 440–41)

CONFLICT

In Heraclitus' view, strife is not an incidental feature of the universe. It is precisely what produces a *kosmos,* an organized world instead of a shapeless mass of stuff. The Greeks made a drink by adding shredded cheese and barley to wine. Only constant, brisk stirring could keep the ingredients from separating, could keep the drink organized as a drink. Heraclitus made that potion his metaphor for the necessity of opposition and conflict in the world. (See Fragment 125.) More literally, he expressed the necessity of strife for the maintenance of the world order by saying "War is father and king of all . . ." and "It is necessary to recognize that war is common and conflict is justice and that all things come to be by conflict" (Fragments 53 and 80).

That war is "common" and that all things happen "according to" conflict are echoes of what Heraclitus said about the *logos* in Fragments 1 and 2. Hence we can now see that the unity of all things, which is proclaimed by the *logos,* consists in every change and every thing being located within, and being regulated by, a system of opposition and conflict.

As was Anaximander, Heraclitus was committed to the idea that no one side of an opposition will be allowed to dominate the other totally or for long. The wisdom and rationality of the world, of nature (of God), dictate an overall balance of power between opposing things. The sequence of changes and the conflicts involved in it proceed, not in a wild and arbitrary fashion, but lawfully, intelligibly.

"Conflict is justice." As was true for Anaximander, here too that pattern of reciprocity in dominance between opposites is good, right. If an organized world is morally desirable, then the strife necessary to produce it is just. Not only is Heraclitus rejecting the typically human desire for the cessation of violence, the belief that it would be a good world were the lion to lay down with the lamb, but he is also attacking a specifically Pythagorean idea. As noted earlier, Pythagoras and his followers held that one member of each pair of opposites, is good and the other evil. In consequence, to establish harmony and beauty in any domain, the good must triumph over the evil, must shape it and control it.

Heraclitus will not accept that. No one opposite (with the exception of "good") is better than any other. All are necessary to what is in fact good: namely that system of order produced by perpetual conflict between things. If one member of an opposition were to dominate permanently, chaos, and not harmony, would result.

Notice that Heraclitus does not deny that harmony is desirable. In a striking turn of events, he speaks of a system of opposed and contending objects as being an attunement or in harmony. Discord is true concord, war is true peace (to borrow a phrase from Orwell's *1984*).

FIRE IN THE COSMOS I

In the preceding sections, I have presented as the core of Heraclitus' thought his attempts to alter (what he identified as) some fundamental human conceptions: especially those about the nature and status of change and about the diversity and relations between features of the world. Treating such conceptual matters, rather than issues about the structure and stuff of the world, as central to his aims makes Heraclitus much more of a philosopher in the modern sense and much less of a scientist.

We now come to a topic that has occupied a large, perhaps disproportionate, amount of the scholarly literature on Heraclitus. Even though we now recognize that he was not, as traditionally believed, a *physicist* in the Milesian manner, still he did hold that the world is, in some sense, constructed out of *fire*. Nor was that merely an incidental idea of his. It was important to Heraclitus that fire be understood to be at the root of the world. The very difficult problem that remains is how we are to understand his claim that the world is made of fire. "The order *(kosmos)* which is common to all was not made by god or man, but it forever was, is and will be: an ever-living fire kindled in measures, going out in measures" (Fragment 30).

That passage is certainly tempting to read as a piece of Ionian cosmology, a temptation no doubt intended by Heraclitus. Many of its themes derived from his predecessors, and some we have already found in Heraclitus. It says that all things share a system of order indestructible and not created by anthropomorphic deeds. The second clause apparently says that the cosmos is composed of fire, which undergoes change regularly and lawfully.

Yet certain features of the fragment indicate that it is not safely read as a sober, standard piece of science. First, *if* (a big if) we take *kosmos* to mean "the present developed world," then to say that it "forever was" is to deny that the world began as a mass of one undifferentiated stuff and only developed organization over time. Yet to deny that is precisely to reject (without argument) the possibility of a cosmogony—which his predecessors regarded as fundamental. Whatever the fragment represents, it is not a *standard* bit of Ionian science. Second, the final clause contains another of Heraclitus' paradoxes: how can an ever-living fire go out? *Sober* science does not aim at such paradoxical assertions.

Textual matters, then, make us hesitant to consider even his most cosmological passages as straightforward science. We also find it difficult to understand how he could think that fire is superior to air (or water) as a candidate for the role of the basic stuff that transforms itself into other stuffs. As Kahn says in his book on Heraclitus, "The point of importance here is that the choice of fire as a substitute for air can scarcely have been motivated by the desire for a more adequate physical theory: nothing is literally derived from fire in the way that winds, clouds and water may be derived from air" (p. 23).

The *physicists* could rationally support their claims that such-and-such stuff could transform into other stuffs by noting what seemed to be facts of nature, natural processes. Water freezes and evaporates, air is sometimes thin, sometimes thick. There is, however, no plausible process by which fire might be held to become water or earth. The lack of reasons for thinking fire would work as the prime cosmic constituent led later Ionian cosmologists to ignore Heraclitus.

FIRE IN THE COSMOS II

Realizing that Heraclitus makes fire central to his account of the world, yet impressed by the serious difficulties in taking fire to be nothing but a theoretical replacement for air in the then current physics, historians of Greek philosophy have discovered another option. Perhaps Heraclitus should not be taken *literally* when he says that the world is fire. Perhaps he was treating fire as a *symbol*, as a piece of *imagery* standing for the basic facts of the world. The care and craft Heraclitus exercised in his writing shows that he had literary ambitions. What would be more natural than for someone with artistic aims to employ imagery describing the world?

That interpretation of the role of fire for Heraclitus had a great deal in its favor. He has held that change is the fundamental category of the universe. What could better represent a world that is perpetually changing than leaping, dancing, shifting flames? Heraclitus wants us to think of change as being a process of conflict, war. What is more destructive than fire, which consumes and destroys whatever it encounters? What an excellent symbol for the violence he finds to be characteristic of the universe!

But interpreting fire as a symbol, while approximating the truth about Heraclitus' aims, is probably not wholly correct either. The contrast between what is symbolic and what is literally true, a contrast the interpretation rests on, would most likely be rejected by Heraclitus as not the entire story. The symbolic and the literal are but another pair of opposites. Between these two, as between the members of all pairs, Heraclitus would presume connection rather than opposition.

What is hard for us to accept is that he did not think in patterns with which we are familiar. Just because there are no *Milesian* (read that as "*scientific*") reasons for making fire the root of the world does not mean that there could be no reasons. The absence of a plausible process by which fire and the other stuffs could interchange may well not have impressed Heraclitus at all. He might have thought that it is reasonable to claim that fire is *literally* the stuff of the world *precisely because* it is a perfect *symbol* of the fundamental aspects of the world. We have already seen that he treats the world as a complicated system of rational discourse, as a linguistic entity. Given that and also given his aim of finding unity in opposites, Heraclitus would have no difficulty in finding that what is symbolic is therefore literally true.

MATTER AND HERACLITUS' MONISM

Even if the preceding suggestions do amount to a correct general view of how we should understand the status of fire in Heraclitus, it certainly does not solve the problems about fire raised by the fragments. Since a resolution of every such difficulty is impossible here anyway, I shall settle for a discussion of a few central issues.

As we have already seen, Heraclitus was a more thorough monist than his Milesian predecessors. He swept up into a single system of cosmic interactions many aspects of the world that the earlier *physicists* had not dreamed of including in their theories: sleeping-waking, hunger-fullness, youth-age— all the opposites, in fact. So when Heraclitus concludes (what is now) Fragment 10 by saying "from all things, one; from one thing, all," that assertion of the unity of all things is seriously intended to cover *all things*.

The comprehensiveness of the view is often difficult to keep in mind. We must especially remember that the system of opposition and conflict is not separate from the stuff of the world. For Heraclitus, gods and dogs and rationality and war-peace are intimately connected (and connected with everything else too), and fire is the root of it all. To emphasize the fundamental role of fire in his account of the universe, some have called Heraclitus a "materialist"; others, who have emphasized that his basic concept is change, have thought it wrong to call him a materialist. Both views are probably partial truths. It is quite possible that Heraclitus' idea might be expressed as follows: change and conflict, *that is to say* fire (or equally, fire, that is to say change and conflict) are found in everything. (It would be improper to think of Heraclitus as a precursor of modern physics. In modern physics, the grounds for asserting the interchangeability of matter and energy are not in the slightest related to whatever reasons Heraclitus may have had for claiming the identity of stuff and change.)

FIRE: VARIATIONS ON THEMES FROM ANAXIMANDER

Heraclitus spoke of the role of fire in much the same terms as Anaximander had of the *apeiron*.

1. First, consider Fragment 64: "Thunderbolt steers all things." Anaximander used (according to Aristotle) the image of a helmsman to characterize the role of the *apeiron* in regulating the world's processes. We have already noticed that Heraclitus appropriates that image (see Fragment 41: "Wisdom is one, knowing the thought by which it steers all things through all things"). Here he deploys that same image, only now speaking of *fire* as that which is in charge of guiding the world's order. Yet he does not blandly say that *fire* plays that role. Rather, he uses the further image of the lightning flash, that bit of heavenly fire with its awesome destructive power, to indicate the regulatory function of fire.

By using the lightning flash as a symbol for fire, he is able to imply the identification of fire with the deity, for lightning was the weapon of Zeus, the chief Homeric god. At the same time, he is able to stress the central place of violence and destruction in the guidance of the world. By now Heraclitus has developed a string of identifications: to the *logos* and wisdom and the entire system of opposites and conflict, he now adds fire as yet another way of specifying the main principle of all things.

2. Anaximander most likely regarded the comings and goings of the cosmic opposites or masses as a process of death and rebirth. The cold slays the hot, later gives birth to it, and will be slain in due course by its child, and so on. Heraclitus, in similarly conceiving the universe to be a locus of continual conflict, also followed Anaximander in describing the cosmic cycles in terms of victory, dominance, and defeat, in terms of death and rebirth. Although Fragment 76 is most certainly muddled in what it claims about cosmological details, the picture it gives of the cosmic stuffs as living and dying in their struggle appears genuinely Heraclitean: "Fire lives the death of earth and air lives the death of fire. . . ."

3. As did Anaximander, Heraclitus believed in a cosmic morality ("Conflict is justice") whereby the advantage of one opposite in a pair or one

form of stuff is merely temporary, to be appropriately redressed when the time is ripe. Fire is the executor and guarantor of justice in the cosmos. In Fragment 16, Heraclitus uses the image of cosmic fire as a never-setting sun to point up its function as moral overseer, and Fragment 66 specifies what fire will do in that role: "How can one escape the notice of that which never sets?" and "Fire will come to all things, to judge and to seize."

4. One hotly disputed question about Heraclitus' views is whether he believed in a great cycle as it seems Anaximander did. Apparently, Anaximander held that there are successive world orders, with a cosmos being reabsorbed back into the *apeiron* every so often. The cosmogonical process would then begin all over with the creation of a new universe. Some evidence exists, though far from conclusive, that Heraclitus told of a similar extended cycle in which, in time, everything goes to its death in a giant cosmic bonfire, with another organized world emerging later.

THE ANTHROPOLOGICAL FRAGMENTS

Historians of Greek philosophy have usually divided Heraclitus' literary remains into two parts, the cosmological fragments and the anthropological. The latter were then relegated to a secondary place in accounts of his views. Heraclitus would have protested that separation of his work into two parts, claiming that in his work, as elsewhere, there is a hidden unity waiting to be discovered. Recent scholarship has tended in that direction, making his writings on human life fall somewhere closer to the center of his philosophical project than allowed by the orthodox interpretation.

Even that last description can be misleading. It presupposes a distinction between people and the world that Heraclitus was almost certainly trying to break down instead. We humans express our relationship to the world as one of opposition: people versus the world we struggle to inhabit. Or, even more narrowly, myself versus all those other things with which I must contend. Characteristically, Heraclitus was intent on rejecting those pieces of opposition by asserting that there is a unity between the self and the cosmos.

HUMAN LIFE AND DEATH

The notion that we, individually and jointly, are but one part of a unified system of nature has led some branches of the recent ecology movement to see Heraclitus as a philosophical ancestor. Both share a vision of the world as a place where individual entities are not the fundamental units of existence, where particular objects are temporary creations of a complex system of exchanges between the living and the nonliving, where everything exists in a perpetually shifting balance of conflicting forces. Moreover, both hold that human beings persistently think and act as if they were not components of the natural order.

Those similarities must not be pushed too far. The background to ecological thought is twentieth-century biological science, allied with concerns about the effects of modern industrial and technological human life on the workings of nature. Heraclitus' views grew out of the rough physics of the Milesians, allied with a concern to understand what happens to us when we die.

What becomes of us at death? Despite the importance of the question for Heraclitus, it is difficult to recognize what his full answer was. It is reasonable to suspect that at least some of the difficulty stems from Heraclitus' intention that his oracular words should be subject to different interpretations. The problematic issue is continuity of personal identity after death. Most, if not all, of the direct evidence (that is, of the relevant fragments) bearing on that question can be read in either of two ways. (It may take considerable intellectual maneuvering to make a given interpretation fit a given piece of evidence.) It can be argued that he held a naturalistic view, denying personal survival of death, or it can be, and has been, argued that he agreed with Pythagoras and allowed for the continued existence of persons, *psychés*, after death.

Heraclitus does not strike me as being in agreement with Pythagoras on this topic (or on any other). It seems to me that interpreting his work as supporting continued existence is contrary to the general spirit of his work and seriously strains the textual evidence as well. Consequently, I shall sketch out a naturalistic account of his position (a reading that also does not fit the evidence perfectly). For a good account of the other interpretation, see Guthrie (1962, Vol. 1, pp. 476–82). Kahn (1979, pp. 210–61) gives a naturalistic answer. Neither would be convinced by the other's arguments. So there is more work to be done.

What, then, *does* become of us at death? First, we must realize that death is a pervasive feature of our lives (a fine Heraclitean paradox). If all things always change and if change is the death of the old and the birth of the new (two doctrines of Heraclitus already discussed), then strictly speaking we have constant experience of death, both our own deaths and the deaths of everything else we encounter. Fragment 21 contains the clause "All that we see when awake is death. . . ." We observe change—death—at every instant in every thing.

Of course, when we asked about our own deaths, those were not the ones we had in mind. Those are, as it were, deaths produced by logic, by employing very strict criteria of identity. What we want to know about is that *major* change that overtakes us, that episode we *ordinarily* speak of as death.

That haste to grasp what happened to *us* is another instance of our human propensity to think we are different from other things found in the world. Before asking about ourselves, we must learn the answer to "What happens to *anything* in due course?" On that subject, Heraclitus had learned from the Milesians a lesson not yet generally available: "Men do not expect or imagine what awaits them at death" (Fragment 27). What people had not yet learned is that *all things* are modifications of one original, incessantly changing, stuff. We human beings must include ourselves in that "all things." That is what Heraclitus wanted to insist on. The stuff we are is the same stuff that has previously, endlessly, been organized into different entities. The clause "All that we see when awake is death . . ." also refers to nature's practice of recycling stuff.

Our fate will be the same as that of those previously created things. Our death is a phase in the cycle. As a different culture expressed it, "Ashes to ashes, dust to dust." Heraclitus' version was, roughly, "from fire to earth, water, and air, and then around again."

PSYCHÉ

Still, a problem remains. Heraclitus can say "A corpse should be flung out like dung" (Fragment 96) and have in mind that our *bodies* will continue through that cycle of transformations. However, what makes what we call our death a unique occurrence among all the other alterations in our lives is that it also entails the disappearance of the principle of life, of the *psyché*. What happens to the *psyché* on our death? The crucial evidence is Fragment 36: "For *psychés* it is death to become water, for water it is death to become earth; from earth comes water and from water, *psyché*." Whatever the details of that story, it is certain that what Heraclitus is there insisting on is that souls are included in the system of material transformations.

He does not, however, hold that *all* souls will die by becoming water. Sufficient evidence shows that Heraclitus held that the souls of most people who live and die *excellently* will not suffer death by becoming moist but will continue to exist as *psyché*-stuff. Scholars dispute whether Heraclitus thought *psyché*-stuff is fire (when we die, we become cold, so the principle of life is related to fire) or air (breath and life are intimately connected). Whichever view is correct, Heraclitus suggests two possible outcomes for those souls who have lived and died *well*; that is, an uncorrupted *psyché* might return to the realm of *psyché*-stuff in one or the other of two ways. Such a *psyché* might rise to become part of the fiery upper air, thereby both literally and figuratively overseeing the processes of transformation occurring below: "[They] rise and become the watchful guardians of life and death" (Fragment 63). Or, since Heraclitus holds that thinking (rationality) is common to all things, the morally upright *psyché* would not be transmuted into other stuffs but would remain as the *psyché*-stuff that exists in everything, that gives everything its share of rationality.

It seems unlikely that Heraclitus thought personal identity survived the loss of the *psyché*-stuff, which loss constitutes our deaths (ordinarily conceived). Surely no continuity persists in the great majority of cases, where a soul changes into water. In cases where a soul is drawn back into the realm of *psyché*-stuff rather than transforming into some other stuff, our rational capacities will continue. That is because the *psyché*, originally only a principle of animation, is now being thought of as the source of thought and reason as well as life.

Yet the belief that our *psychés* as rational capacities survive our deaths most likely meant for Heraclitus that our *psyché*-stuff would lose those private, unique, idiosyncratic features of a soul that makes for personal identity, identity as a particular person (a view Aristotle also later defended). Through Heraclitus runs a disparagement of what is private to an individual, especially of what is intellectually one's own. (For Heraclitus these ideas are not his own: the *logos* is speaking *through* him.) His disapproval of thinking that reason is something personal derives from his claim that the *logos* is shared, hence not at all private to any individual. ". . . [Al]though the *logos* is common to all, most men live as though their thinking were private" (Fragment 2). The return of a given bit of *psyché*-stuff to the fold after temporary assignment to a human life would mean the loss of what was unique to that particular placement.

RELIGIOUS BELIEF AND PRACTICE

Heraclitus took over and extended Xenophanes' critique of traditional religion. Not only do people have a wrong—that is, an anthropomorphic—conception of the gods, but that misconception also leads them to engage in undesirable and irrational religious practices in worship of gods so conceived. "They pray to these statues as though talking to a house, not understanding what gods and heroes [demigods] are like" (Fragment 5).

Despite his rejection of conventional religious belief and practice, Heraclitus, like Xenophanes, did not respond to the deficiencies in that religion, as did the Pythagoreans and other mystery cults of the time. Initiations, rites, orgies, even *theoria,* all were practiced as means of overcoming the separation of human and god, as techniques for achieving salvation. From Heraclitus' point of view, all such activities are pointless as means to those ends precisely because those ends are unattainable. It is not in human power to escape the circle of destruction and rebirth.

What is more, we already enjoy the desired union with the gods, are already one with them. As with all other oppositions in the world, Heraclitus takes the contrast between the human and the divine to be not ultimate, to hide a unity. A most famous fragment is 62: "Immortals are mortal, mortals are immortal, living the other's death, dying in their life." Heraclitus not only claims, in a sense, our immortality, but he does so by denying, in a sense, the immortality of the gods. Stuffs of which the world is composed are immortal, undying, but at the same time they are capable of being transformed—that is, of dying—into those things we normally think of as mortal creations. But even those mortals, since they are composed of stuff that is endlessly recycled, are in that way immortal.

It must be remembered that over and above those gods and immortals mentioned in the preceding paragraphs, Heraclitus held that there is one supreme god. That leading god he identifies with a number of key notions: with the *logos*, with cosmic justice and wisdom, with war and with fire, in fact with the entire pattern of conflict and change in the universe. "Heraclitus' god is neither personal nor transcendent; it is wholly immanent in the world and identical with the order of the cosmos over time" (Kahn, 1979, p. 267).

OTHER PHILOSOPHICAL ISSUES

Early Greek inquiry, much of which we today speak of as Pre-Socratic philosophy, was overwhelmingly occupied with problems that, in different ways, centered on the world in which we live. With time, different kinds of philosophical questions came to be asked. For instance, it was natural to follow the initial cosmological concerns with questions about the gods and their place in the order of things. Pythagoras and Heraclitus added still another range of issues: what is the relation of human beings to the cosmos?

Only very slowly, however, was philosophical attention given to questions of human relations, to what we today would call political and moral philosophy. The Pythagoreans show some beginnings of interest in those matters. Heraclitus adds a little to that. He commends (what is usually translated as) *moderation* as the highest excellence or virtue, a thought that does not go much beyond the wisdom of the Sages. He also had sayings pertaining to political life, especially to the necessity of citizens defending the laws of their city. Those fragments raise some interesting problems concerning the compatibility of that value with his assertion of the necessity and value of strife and conflict. Pursuing those issues here, however, would misrepresent their overall importance in his thought.

One other kind of issue must be looked into before concluding a discussion of Heraclitus. Xenophanes had raised a new and philosophically important type of question, namely, one about our *knowledge* of the world. He suggested that we would never be able to arrive at knowledge and would have to content ourselves with belief. Insofar as he gave any thought to the question of *how* such ideas as we have about the world are to be attained and justified, Xenophanes would probably have talked about the use of our *senses*.

Heraclitus, however, had no qualms about the possibility of our knowing how things are. And he made a significant contribution to the question of how we are to be justified in our claims that the world is this way rather than that.

We saw earlier that Heraclitus commended the senses over and against the pronouncements of authority. But we also saw that he said "Eyes and ears make bad witnesses if men cannot understand the language." That is, learning the facts of the world via our senses is not sufficient. In order to *make something* of, to understand, what our senses tell us, it is necessary to exercise our rational capacities, to *reason*.

Over and over again, Heraclitus emphasizes the role of reason in the universe and in our apprehension of that world. For instance, the Milesian claim that only one kind of stuff underlies the diversity of objects was not based on the senses; rather, the origins, history, and constitution of the world were rationally inferred. Again, it is not our senses that show us everything is always changing; the constancy of change is not observed but inferred.

A distinction between what we learn by the senses and what we learn by reason was implicit in the Milesian cosmogonies and cosmologies. Reflections by the Pythagoreans and others on the nature of mathematics also contributed to a growing appreciation of the function of reason in the new forms in inquiry. It was Heraclitus who first began making all that explicit, who began to emphasize that (1) how the world really is differs from how it looks to the senses and (2) therefore, claims about how it really is rest, at least to a considerable extent, on reason.

HERACLITUS AS PHILOSOPHER

Contemporary philosophers find a major anomaly in Heraclitus' work that is worth noticing here in conclusion. On the one hand, he stressed the use of reason in comprehending the world. Yet the extensive fragments are wholly lacking in what the philosophical tradition since his time came to regard as the major display of rationality. No one single *argument* appears in the fragments, and we have no reason to believe that any appeared in the original book. His sayings were just that, sayings, the rational basis of which he left the reader to construct. That lack of argument, plus his allusive literary style, makes Heraclitus simultaneously fascinating (he presents us with so many puzzles to solve) and yet an outsider, someone who did not really do philosophy, did not play the rational game.

At least we can be fairly certain of a partial way to explain the absence of any attempt to prove what he was saying or to be clear about it. Although original in *what* he had to say, he made no attempt at originality in the perspective from which he wrote. In fact, he reverted to a framework older than the new forms of thinking and writing that grew out of Ionian inquiry. He wrote as a wise man, as a sage. He modeled himself on the Delphic oracle. From such elevated perspectives, rational support of what one has to say may well seem unnecessary. In consequence, Heraclitus seems to the modern philosopher much less a philosophical figure than the next thinker in the historical succession.

BIBLIOGRAPHY

Charles H. Kahn, *The Art and Thought of Heraclitus* (Cambridge, England: Cambridge University Press, 1979).

An excellent book, certain to dominate discussions of Heraclitus for years. It is also very accessible to the nonspecialist.

PARMENIDES I:
THE ANALYSIS OF BEING

Thales, the first of the Pre-Socratics, was born about 624 B.C.E.; Parmenides *(Par-men'-eh-deez)*, about 515. Thus we have now covered a full century in the development of philosophical and scientific thought.

Parmenides, however, represents vastly more than the beginning of a second century of philosophy. Everyone agrees that he is *philosophically* the most important Pre-Socratic, that he undermined previous cosmological work, that his conclusions extensively redirected the scientific movement, and that he not only had original things to say but also argued in an original manner for those views.

To grasp the nature of Parmenides' achievement, we must look beyond the impact he had on his own time. He has, for instance, an effect on twentieth-century readers unlike that of any other Pre-Socratic. Even introductory students want to *argue* with Parmenides, in ways and to an extent that they would not respond to the views of other Pre-Socratics. The reaction of modern philosophers is the same. Thus the *type* of intellectual activity engaged in by Parmenides was something new, was of a kind that makes him more alive to us than are the other historically important early philosophers.

It is easier to note the uniqueness of Parmenides among the Pre-Socratics than to adequately characterize what makes him unique. Let me settle for naming the situation. With significant apologies to Heraclitus, let me say that Parmenides was the first *metaphysician*.

One of Plato's most important and difficult dialogues is known as the *Parmenides*. In it he "reports" on the meeting of the young Socrates with the famous Parmenides, then aged about sixty-five, who has come to Athens, along with his disciple Zeno, for a festival. From Plato's remarks, such a meeting would have occurred shortly after 450 B.C.E., making Parmenides' birth about 515. When he died is unknown—sometime after 450 B.C.E.

He was a native and resident of the *polis* of Elea on the western coast of Italy. Like many of his fellow philosophers, he was probably active in the political life of his city. There are rumors that he had some connection with

Xenophanes, who spent many years in that part of the Greek world. More important are the reports of his having been a Pythagorean while young. Elea was close to Croton and the other centers of Pythagorean influence in southern Italy. Moreover, internal evidence in his writing shows that Parmenides did know Pythagorean ideas. If that is true, his work would be, in part, a dissent from Pythagoreanism.

A Procedural Warning

Before starting an examination of Parmenides, I need to say something about how I will conduct that examination. Up to this point in my discussions of the Pre-Socratics, I have largely attempted to report on their views at a rather high level of generality. I have not, that is, tried to explore and explain their views in detail. With Parmenides, I must change tactics, and the contrast may rudely shock some readers. Hence I need to account for the obviously different manner in which Parmenides will be discussed.

I have already said that Parmenides created a new type of philosophical activity, one labeled "metaphysics" but that might also have been called "professional philosophy" (or "hard-core philosophy"). For those uninitiated into that activity, whether they were Parmenides' contemporaries or whether they are moderns, when confronted with a piece of professional metaphysics, it is tough going to grasp what is going on and why. *The only hope of understanding and appreciating Parmenides (or any other such hard-core philosopher) is to be willing to talk through the issues and arguments in detail.* Consequently, *any* helpful presentation of Parmenides' views must deal with details. The following account, while it does not make understanding Parmenides easy, aims at exploring his work thoroughly enough to give those who are willing to make the effort a fighting chance at comprehending what he was doing and why.

PARMENIDES' POEM

Parmenides' philosophical writing took the form of a poem. About 160 lines, including a few fragmentary ones, of that poem still exist. The introduction or prologue has survived complete. Scholars estimate that we possess about 90 percent of the most important section of the poem, conventionally known as the Way of Truth, but perhaps only 10 percent of the less important section called the Way of Appearance. What does remain of the entire poem gives us today a higher percentage of Parmenides' total work than of any other Pre-Socratic.

The poem, presumably written before Parmenides acquired fame and disciples, is in hexameters, the versification scheme employed by writers of epics (Homer, Hesiod, and others). He is thus to be located, in literary terms, within the epic tradition, which distinguishes him from (1) the Ionians, who rejected the poetic past in their invention of the prose treatise, and (2) Heraclitus, whose affinities were with oracular and aphoristic literature. It is a very debated question as to how bad a poet Parmenides was. It is agreed that his poem is not a success poetically, that it is not a classic of Greek literature (although it is now recognized that Parmenides had a good ear for language and relished Heraclitean word play).

Its large poetic failures are certainly due, in part, to Parmenides' shortcomings as a writer of verse. More significantly, though, the poem does not succeed as poetry because the new, and very intellectual, wine he attempted to put into the epic bottle was not suitable for that type of container. What is proper for storytelling does not work for presenting abstract deductive argument.

The Prologue

The bulk of the poem, including its philosophical matter, consists of a speech by an unnamed goddess. That speech is prefaced by the following passage:

> The mares which carry me to what I desire brought me to the Sun's path, that famous highway which carries the man who knows above every city. Along that road I was carried by the wise horses, drawing at full speed the chariot, driven by the daughters of the Sun. The axle, whirled round by the wheels, blazed and sang in the sockets as the goddesses, pulling the veils from their faces left the house of Night and hastened me toward the light.
>
> The paths of Night and Day are blocked by gates, extending high into the air and framed by a lintel and a stone threshold. The great doors with their double bolts are controlled by avenging Justice. The maidens plied her with gentle words and skillfully persuaded her to release the bolts without delay. Pivoting on bronze pins, the doors flew open to create a wide entry-way. Straight through and along the broad road the maidens guided the horses and chariot.
>
> The goddess kindly received me, took my right hand in hers and spoke these words to me: "Young man who has been escorted to my house by immortal charioteers, I welcome you. It is not evil that has set you to travel this way, far from the beaten track of men, but both right and justice. It is proper for you to learn all things: both the unchanging heart of complete truth and also how things seem to mortals, in which there is no truth. Despite that lack of truth, you must learn how what seems to be must be because it is accepted." (Fragment 1)

Then the goddess immediately begins her account of "the unchanging heart of complete truth."

By putting his philosophical views in the mouth of a goddess, Parmenides is claiming for them the status of divine revelation. In doing that he is partially following Homer and Hesiod, who begin their epic tales by invoking the assistance of the Muses. Nonetheless, by having the goddess directly speak the words, Parmenides claims considerably more than mere divine *inspiration.*

How did these matters come to be revealed to him? It was the result of a journey "far from the beaten track of men." He had journeyed from darkness ("the house of Night") to light ("the Sun's path"), an allegory or metaphor (we would say) meaning, then as now, an advance from ignorance to enlightenment. In following the route of "the man who knows," he was given divine assistance, and both justice and the goddess who receives him confirm his right to be there, to learn the truth.

In her introductory remarks the goddess tells Parmenides that "learning all things" consists in studying two different subject matters. First, he must learn the truth. He must also learn "how things seem to mortals in which there is no truth." I have mentioned that the body of the poem divides into two parts, conventionally called the Way of Truth and the Way of Appearance (or Seeming). Those parts correspond to the two lessons the goddess promises. She begins, and so we too, with the Way of Truth.

The Structure and Outcome of the Way of Truth

Having tried to make sense of the earlier Pre-Socratics when so little of their writing has survived may make it seem a pure blessing to have so much of the central part of Parmenides' poem to work with. And of course the extensive fragments are welcome. However, having more presents its own problems. Translating and understanding Parmenides' poem, especially in its details, is extremely difficult. Scholarly consensus is no greater on deciding the fine points in Parmenides than it is on interpreting his predecessors.

Yet the broad outlines of what Parmenides was doing, at least in the Way of Truth, are very clear. That section of the poem consists of two projects. First Parmenides argues for a thesis. Then he makes clear a set of shocking consequences of accepting that thesis.

This is not a detective story, so it is appropriate to reveal at the start the conclusions Parmenides came to. (Knowing where he is going may well help the reader better follow the twists of the argument.) Parmenides first argues that we human beings are wrong in thinking that there is any such thing as possibility in the world. What is *has to* be, and what is not *cannot* be. But even that won't do; he argues that it makes no sense to talk about what is not. All that we can intelligibly think and say is that things are. That is the outcome of his first project. His second aim is to derive the consequences of that initial conclusion. There are many consequences, all shocking. The chief ones are that the world consists of only one object, that that one item of worldly furniture has no properties, and that it cannot have come into being or pass away or change in any other respect. Lastly and obviously, there is small prospect for conducting scientific inquiries, given the nature of what is.

Parmenides does not pronounce those things—he is not in the slightest a mystic or a prophet. He rigorously *argues* that that is how things are. To understand Parmenides, it is necessary to grasp *why* he holds the views he does.

THE TEXT

We will, of course, begin our study of the Way of Truth with the first leg of his program, the proof of his fundamental truth. I have combined four separate fragments, as follow, that compose most of what remains of the first half of the Way of Truth. Fragment 2 certainly came immediately after the Prologue and is thus the opening of the account of Truth. Fragment 3 most likely is the final clause of what we call Fragment 2. Again, Fragments 6 and 8 probably form a single unit. I have made them continuous with the other two pieces, although that may not be where they occurred in the original poem.

The following version of these fragments papers over a number of disagreements concerning the proper translation, at least some of which must be discussed later. The reader should attempt to obtain a general grasp of the passage this time through, leaving the ensuing discussion to settle questions of precise meaning.

> Come now, I will tell you—and you must tell others—the only conceivable ways of thinking. The first, that it is and it must be, is the persuasive way for it goes with truth. The other way of thinking, that it is not and it cannot be, is wholly impossible. That is impossible because you cannot know what is not nor can you express it [Fragment 2], for it is the same thing which can be thought and which can be [Fragment 3].
>
> What you can speak of and think of has to be, since it can be while nothing cannot be. Think about that. For that is the first way of thinking from which I hold you back. I also hold you back from that way on which mortals, knowing nothing, wander two-headed, helplessness guiding their wandering minds. They go along, both deaf and blind, in a daze, creatures without judgment, who think that to be and not to be are the same yet not the same and that the way of all things turns upon itself [Fragment 6]. For this shall never be proved; that things that are not are. So do not take that way of thinking. Do not let your habits, born of long experience, force your thoughts in that direction, to travel with an aimless eye, a droning ear and tongue. Rather judge by your reason the contentious refutation I have spoken [Fragment 7].

Interpretive problems arise immediately with that passage. The core of the poem begins with a reference to what is literally translatable as "ways of seeking, of searching." Most translators render that into English as "ways of *inquiry*," relying on a connection between seeking for something and inquiring into something. The consequence of that translation (probably its intent) is that Parmenides is immediately assimilated to his predecessors through the idea of inquiry.

Yet he did not use their word, *historie*, as he could have had he wanted to align himself with their concerns and outlook. As he went so far as to invent a new word for what *he* is talking about, it is safest not to think of him as concerned with *inquiry,* at least not after we have appropriated that word for his predecessors' activities.

What he does seem to have in mind are ways of thinking about things, the ways in which we conceive of and talk about things. Hence my translation "ways of *thinking*."

Parmenides says that he will point out the *conceivable* ways of thinking. Whereas Fragment 2 gives the distinct impression that only two such ways exist, Fragment 6 makes it clear that there is yet another. He thus holds that there are *three* possible modes of thought about things.

His initial aim in the Way of Truth can now be more precisely specified. He was out to establish a major thesis: although there are, formally speaking, three conceivable ways to think about things, on investigation two of those will actually turn out to be impossible. Hence Parmenides believes that one and only one possible way exists of conceiving of things. That one survivor functions as the premise for conclusions drawn in the second of the two projects that constitute the Way of Truth.

The three ways are (1) the one that will survive the process of elimination is "it is and it must be"; (2) a way that will turn out to be "wholly impossible" is "it is not and cannot be"; and (3) a third way (also impossible), belatedly mentioned and rejected in Fragment 6 without ever being as clearly stated as the first two. One central task of the following commentary will be to provide a much more detailed characterization of that somewhat mysterious third way.

"It"

Anyone who has not worked through Parmenides before will be asking some highly reasonable questions by now, the most important of which is "What in the world is going on?" What, despite the hints, is "a way of thinking"? What is meant by that talk about "it is" and "it is not" and so on? The next step must be a clarification of some of these troubles. Let us begin with the subject pronoun.

What the "it" in Parmenides' formulas refers to has been *the* scholarly question about this part of the poem. The text provides no obvious antecedent for the pronoun (no wonder readers lose their bearings). Consequently, differences of opinion arise as to how to understand what Parmenides is talking about.

Of the several options offered by the history of thought about Parmenides (which includes the idea that "'it' lacks a subject, as in "It is raining"), the most popular has become "What is." That does have some virtues and so cannot be lightly dismissed, but it has even more serious flaws. There is no textual evidence that Parmenides intended that, or any other, *definite* reading of the pronoun's reference. Furthermore, if he had meant that, he could easily have said so, could in fact have very powerfully asserted the first two ways of thought to be "What is, is" and "What is not, is not." Yet he didn't. Lastly, so interpreted, the "it" requires a different subject in each of the two ways—"what is" in the first and "what is not" in the other. Yet those "ways" seem to be options concerning one and the same thing, something picked out by "it."

There is a better way to consider Parmenides' use of the pronoun "it." He uses the word "it" from the beginning and continues to do so throughout the Way of Truth. He does not attempt to fill in the blank. Yet he must have known that the question "What is the *it* that is (and so on)?" is askable and would surely be asked. We must conclude that the openness produced by his use of the pronoun (or the equivalent device in his Greek)—his failure to be specific—was intended. He said "it" because he meant *it*.

It is possible to make sense of his practice only if we regard the correct answer to "What is the it?" as "*Whatever.*" That is, Parmenides did not further specify the subject of the pronoun because it refers to *anything that can be thought of or mentioned*. He did not have in mind some particular thing or things. Rather, he was talking about anything whatsoever.

What Parmenides needed was the notion of a *variable*. (In the algebraic formula, "$2x = y$," the symbols x and y are variables: they don't specify particular numbers, as does 2.) At the time, no one, not even mathematicians, had a clear-cut understanding of what a variable is. What he was trying to say, in the terminology of modern logic, is that "x is and x must be," "x is not and x cannot be" where the variable x ranges over whatever objects can be thought of, spoken of.

"Is"

In the process of clarifying what Parmenides meant in calling "it is" a "way of thought," one item requiring clarification is the *verb*. In fact, the meaning of the verb in his formulas is very important.

The verb *to be* is central to Parmenides' philosophical investigations—he talks about "it *is* and it must *be*," "it *is not* and it cannot *be*" and, in his account of the third way, says, "*to be* and *not to be* are the same yet not the same."

In light of his concern with the verb *to be*, it is possible to describe Parmenides as inquiring into *Being*. His "ways of thought" can then be thought of as possible ways in which we can think of Being.

Philosophers today say that there are three ways in which the word *is* (and other forms of *to be*) are used. It can be used as equivalent to "exists." Hamlet's famous "To be or not to be?" is certainly a question about existence. The question "Do dinosaurs exist?" is more naturally phrased in terms of the verb *to be* (namely as "*Are* there dinosaurs?") and the answer "There *aren't* any" denies their existence.

The second "is" is today called the "is" of *predication*. We say not only "Socrates is" but also "Socrates is wise" ("fascinating, pudgy, tough," and so on), and we thus use "is" as a copula, as a connector, hooking up a subject term with a predicate. So too denials are linguistically possible with this "is": "She is not very cheerful," "Snails are not good companions."

The final use of the word "is" is usually referred to by contemporary philosophers as the "is" of *identity*. We can use the word "is" not only to assert existence or the possession of a property, and so on, but also to indicate the *sameness* or *difference* of things. We say things such as "Clark Kent *is* Superman" and mean that the person called by the one name *is identical with* the person called by the other name. We also deny identity: "That man is not (the same person as) the one who robbed me." We use the "is" of identity to hold that one thing is or is not the same as something named or described or identified differently.

As Parmenides was concerned with Being, with the verb "to be," which of those different uses of "is" did he have in mind? The correct answer is "All of them." Parmenides himself would not have been in a position to say that there are different senses of "is" covered by his arguments and views. He no doubt realized that "is" occurs in different linguistic contexts, but it would not have occurred to *anyone* at that time that there are significant differences in the meaning of "is" as it occurs in different contexts. Yet if we are to make sense of Parmenides' conclusions, we must hold him to have known that we make existence statements and predications and claims about identity with the word "is."

Most interpreters have treated Parmenides as concerned with *existence* claims. That is, when he lays out the conceivable modes of thought, he is taken to be asserting that, with respect to its existence, we might say three things of an object, namely that it *exists* (and must) or that it does not *exist* (and cannot), or something that amounts to saying that *existing* and *not existing* are the same yet not the same.

More recent scholarship has made it clear that Parmenides saw his formulas as applicable to the "is" of predication. I will go even further and set out his argument in such a way that the "is" of identity becomes crucial. Nonetheless, the best way to begin working through Parmenides' position, and through his arguments in support of it, is to interpret the various occurrences of "to be" in the Way of Truth to mean "to exist." However, in the long run the verb must *also* be interpreted in other ways if we are to understand Parmenides fully. The "is" in "Socrates is ill" and that in "The teacher of Plato is Socrates" (neither of which can be paraphrased as "exists") are as much subject to Parmenides' arguments as is the "is" of "Socrates is (exists)."

Consequently, we shall initially regard those first two ways of thinking as "it exists and it must exist" and "it does not exist and it cannot exist." The third way will also be specifiable in terms of existence. Later, having worked through the relevant parts of the poem with that interpretation in mind, we will have to extend our attention to other uses of the verb "to be."

Modality and the Ways of Thinking

Given the additional understanding we have now gained, let us return to the topic of "ways of thinking" and try to grasp what Parmenides was up to. This time the inquiry can be best conducted by looking into what he says about the ways of thinking.

Parmenides says the first two ways consist of two clauses apiece: "It is *and* it must be" and " It is not *and* it cannot be." Most explanations of his meaning concentrate overwhelmingly on the first clauses and largely, if not wholly, ignore the second. Yet the second conjuncts are the keys to understanding Parmenides.

Those second clauses have been translated here as "It must be" (or "It has to be") and "It cannot be." However, we all know that what must be (what has to be) is the same as what is *necessary* and that talk of what cannot be is talk of what is *impossible*. Hence the translations of the second conjuncts could equally have been "It is necessary for it to be" and "It is impossible for it to be."

Let me introduce some technical terminology. In philosophy today, the (perfectly ordinary and everyday) concepts of *necessity* and *impossibility* are called *modal* concepts. A third important modal notion is related to those two: that of *possibility*. Possibility covers such phrases as "It is possible," "It can be," "maybe," "perhaps," "probably."

Parmenides, then, partially characterized each of the first two ways of thinking in terms of modal concepts: the first way involves the notion of necessity; the second, the concept of impossibility. Moreover, I shall be maintaining that the third of his ways of thinking is best seen as involving the third modal notion, that of possibility. There are exactly three conceivable modes of thought in Parmenides' scheme just because there are exactly three modal concepts.

PARMENIDES AS LOGICIAN

If one looks carefully at the fragments translated earlier, it is striking how frequently modal ideas turn up in them. Noticing that feature of Parmenides' thought leads to an understanding of the kind of philosophical activity he was engaged in. His first and fundamental interest, however strange this may seem, was in those modal concepts, in the logical relationships they have, both to each other and to other notions.

That interest marks Parmenides off decisively from his predecessors. They were fundamentally interested in the structure and history of the universe, although some were even more concerned with the religious and human lessons to be learned from that scientific endeavor. Parmenides' point of departure, however, is not cosmology, nor does he worry about the implications of cosmology for the conduct of human life. Rather, his problems—what he thinks about—have to do with certain *concepts* and their *logical implications and relationships*. If the other Pre-Socratics are the prototypes of today's scientists and of those who discuss the human implications of science, then Parmenides is the proto*logician*.

In taking up an investigation of certain *conceptual questions*, Parmenides became the ultimate ancestor of what has come to be one of the central types of philosophical activity. Although it is striking to discover the originator of a wholly new type of intellectual interest, it is not surprising that Parmenides engaged in that new style of inquiry in connection with the modal concepts. If, as there is good evidence for, he did begin his intellectual career among the Pythagoreans, he was there exposed to sophisticated mathematical thought. One clear and obvious feature of mathematical discussion is frequent use of the various modal notions. For instance, an early mathematical discovery was that the result of multiplying any integer by 2 *has to be* an even number. A more complicated realization was that it is *impossible* to construct a right triangle whose hypotenuse is shorter than either of the other two sides. Even possibility is easily spotted in mathematicians' talks: "*Can* (say) 2,372 be divided by 3 without remainder?"

Very probably, Parmenides' interest in modal concepts arose from his exposure to the frequent use of those notions in the mathematical work of the Pythagoreans. The conceptual investigations into which that interest led him not only comprise the core of his philosophical thought but were also the first such investigations in what turned out to be a central form of philosophical enterprise.

WHAT MODAL STATEMENTS ENTAIL

Parmenides' philosophical thought began in an interest in modality and in logical relationships entered into by the modal concepts. In particular, he inquired into what follows about how the world is from a modal statement and, conversely, what follows modally from a statement about how the world is. Let us start with the first topic, what modal statements entail, because Parmenides' conclusions about that are clear.

Suppose first that it is necessary that there is a man named Socrates. What follows about Socrates' existence? Clearly, if it is necessary for him to exist, then it logically follows that he does exist. To generalize, if something has to be so, then it *is* so. (Example: If the keys *have to be* here, then they *are* here.)

Turn now to the concept of impossibility. What logical connection exists between (1) the impossibility of something and (2) whether or not that thing is so? Suppose, for example, that Socrates *cannot* exist. Clearly, then he does not exist. (If the keys truly *cannot be* on the table, then they *are not* there.) That is, the impossibility of something requires that the thing is not so.

What about the analogous social implications of the third modal concept, possibility? Here the story is quite different., for there is no analog. From the possibility that Socrates exists, it cannot legitimately be inferred either that he does exist or that he does not. For of course, the possibility of his existing leaves open the possibility of his not existing. To generalize: that something is possible (such as that the Angels will win the pennant) does not logically require either that it is or is not so (that they will win or will not win).

In sum, knowing how the world must be, or how it cannot be, tells you how it is, but knowing how it *might* be does not settle the question of how it is.

WHAT ENTAILS MODAL STATEMENTS

The preceding claims concern what inferences can legitimately be made from modal assertions to assertions about how the world is. Those relationships, being straightforward, were worked out and recognized by Parmenides once he had begun reflecting on the modal concepts.

In attempting to explain his stating the first two ways of thinking as compound propositions ("It is *and* it must be," "It is not *and* it cannot be"), we must conclude that he also tried to determine what the logical connections are in the opposite direction. That is, he wanted to see what modal assertions can be inferred from assertions about how the world is. Not only did he certainly make the attempt, but he also thereby arrived at views that are absolutely at the heart of his philosophical system.

In contrast to the investigation just recorded, Parmenides started this inquiry from assertions about how things are and then looked to discover what, if any, modal implications those have. Broadly speaking, three sorts of things can be said about how things are. For instance, what are the ways in which we can think about Socrates' existence? We can think first that there *is* such a person ("It is") or, second, that there is not ("It is not"). Over and above those primary ways of thinking, those types of assertion, is a third, somewhat heterogeneous, class of things we can and do say when faced with issues of how things are, things that in different ways hedge our bets or otherwise qualify our assertions. For example, we might say, "I don't know" ("have no idea," and so on) "whether (say) Socrates exists." Or we can say, "Well, he doesn't exist—but he used to." At one time in Socrates' life it could have been said, "He exists, but he won't tomorrow." For reasons to be seen later, I am lumping this somewhat diverse group of ways of talking together as a third way of responding to questions about how things are.

Now, given those three possible starting places, Parmenides came to the following conclusions. It logically follows from a proposition that something is, such as that Socrates exists, that it must be—that (say) Socrates must exist. Furthermore, if something is not, then it is logically necessary that it cannot be: if Socrates does not exist, then it is logically necessary that it cannot be: if Socrates does not exist, there cannot be such a person.

Here it is worth observing that precisely those two conclusions cause the radically unorthodox views Parmenides came to hold. Put another way, to reject Parmenides' ultimate theses about what is, and about what it is like, and about change, requires rejecting just those two conclusions. We do not ordinarily think that if something is that it must therefore be, or that what is not cannot be. Any critical inquiry into Parmenides' philosophical views must attempt to understand why he thought that he was right (and we are wrong) about those particular logical relationships.

Why did he reach those conclusions? No words of his own on the topic have been preserved. I presume that Parmenides argued as follows: Suppose we start with the thought that "It is"—for example, that Socrates exists. This surely means "He has to exist," for if an existing thing does not *have* to exist, it could be nonexistent; but being both an existing thing and yet nonexistent is contradictory and so impossible. Hence, Socrates' existence is incompatible with the possibility of his not existing. If something exists, it must exist.

One can fashion a parallel argument about the second alternative: that Socrates does not exist. Suppose that he does not exist. If so, that *must be* how things are. Otherwise, something nonexistent might nonetheless exist—but that cannot be. So what does *not* exist cannot exist. To say that Socrates "doesn't exist but he might exist" is contradictory. If something does *not* exist, it cannot possibly exist.

Something like those arguments (misguided though they are) must have been behind Parmenides' conclusions that what is must be and what is not cannot be.

To pick up the thread of the discussion: So far nothing has been said of that third group of ways of commenting on the existence of something. In response to "Does Socrates exist?" one can say not only "He does" or "He does not" but also, for instance, "I don't know." The important thing to notice here—and Parmenides must have been well aware of it—is that the "I don't know" answer, and others of this group, commit the speaker to the belief that it is *possible* that Socrates exists and *also possible* that he does not. Parmenides was probably less interested in the "I don't know" answers than in others of the group; for example, "He used to but no longer does," "He does but will cease to someday." All those also accept that it is possible for a thing to be and possible for it not to be. In short, members of this third group of responses all connect up with the concept of possibility.

PRELIMINARY SUMMARY

So far, the results of reconstructing Parmenides' thinking are these: he found that "It is necessary that it is" entails "It is" and that "It is" entails "It is necessary to be." That is, how things are and how they must be came to be thought of by Parmenides as *equivalent*. And so we get his first way of thinking: "It is and it must be." Even "It is" by itself will do since one who says that *must mean* "it must be."

Similarly, the arguments seem to establish an *equivalence* between "It is not" and "It is impossible for it to be." Thus he arrives at his second way of thought: "It is not and cannot be" or just "It is not."

The third modal concept, possibility, does not entail any assertion about how things are, and conversely, any assertion such as "I have no idea" or "Things were different" or "Things will be different" leads back to the concept of possibility.

Parmenides' first aim in the Way of Truth was to establish the following: For any object that can be thought of, imagined, there are three conceivable ways of thinking of it with respect to whether it is (taken for now as meaning whether it exists). We must either say that it is, it exists, and to say *that*

(Parmenides has been held to argue) is the same as saying it must exist; or we can maintain that it does not exist and *that* (he holds) commits us to thinking of it as something that cannot exist. Or we may offer a range of answers that commit us to regarding the thing not as a necessary or impossible existent but as a possible existent.

FROM CATALOGING TO CRITICISM

We have now followed Parmenides through the first phase of his first project. He takes himself as having given a complete inventory of the conceivable responses to a question that can be asked of any object we can think of, namely "Is it?" (which we are presently interpreting as "Does it exist?"). Moreover, in compiling that inventory, he has argued that each of the potential responses has very distinctive connections to one or another of the three modal concepts.

In the second stage of his project, Parmenides will examine the three conceivable responses to determine whether they are legitimate. We will see that Parmenides finds only one of the three a genuine possibility, an intelligible way of thinking of the existence of anything. He will provide arguments designed to eliminate two of the candidates.

Before taking up those arguments, it is important to reflect on this new direction of Parmenides' inquiry. So far, his aim has been *descriptive,* merely to catalog the possible ways of thinking of a thing's existence and the relations between those and the modal concepts. But now Parmenides, in going on to characterize some of those possibilities as illegitimate, as unintelligible, will no longer be describing. In attempting to eliminate some and commend others, he will be taking sides, *prescribing* how we must think if we are to think intelligibly and truly. And since we humans accept one of those ways of thought that he brands illegitimate, he will be *criticizing* how we think.

THE THIRD WAY

In his own ordering of the arguments, Parmenides disposes of the second way before he even mentions the other unacceptable way of regarding the existence of things. For our purposes, it will be best to reverse that order of criticism and to examine first his rejection of the third way. Everything he has to say on that topic is given in the following words:

> I also hold you back from that way on which mortals, knowing nothing, wander two-headed, helplessness guiding their wandering minds. They go along, both deaf and blind, in a daze, creatures without judgment, who think that to be and not to be are the same yet not the same and that the way of all things turns upon itself [Fragment 6]. For this shall never be proved: that things that are not are. So do not take that way of thinking. Do not let your habits, born of long experience, force your thought in that direction, to travel with an aimless eye, a droning ear

and tongue. Rather judge by your reason the contentious refutation I have spoken [Fragment 7].

Compared with the manner in which Parmenides eliminates the second way, this passage is notable both for its length and for the scorn he heaps on this way of regarding existence. Two different reasons explain those features of the passage: first, he genuinely believes this to be an absurd way to think; yet, second, it is precisely how we "mortals" do talk and think about the existence of objects.

Recall that Parmenides never characterizes this mode of thought as precisely as he does the other two. The reason for that omission is fairly clear: since he is here discussing how we all think, there seems no special need to describe it in detail—he thinks we are perfectly familiar with it. However, even though we do know it full well, our understanding of Parmenides' position will be enormously assisted by reminding ourselves of just what we say and think about the existence of things. So I will set out those features of our ordinary thought and talk about existence with which Parmenides was concerned.

Of some things (say, polar bears and mountains), we think and say that they exist. Of others, we deny that they exist: there is no free lunch and no Santa Claus. About still others, we don't know whether they exist or not (such as the ski mittens I lost three years ago, Howard Hughes's final will, an inhabited planet in the next galaxy.) We think it possible such things exist, but we also think it possible that they may not.

Yet another group of ideas must be noticed. We think that, of those things that do exist, it is possible for them not to exist. For example, each of us might never have existed. In fact, every(?) object that does exist came into existence at some time and will later pass out of existence. Conversely, those things that do not exist (except contradictory objects such as round squares) might have existed (such as Santa Claus) or might come to exist (such as my tenth child). Moreover, many things that do not exist have done so in the past although they no longer do so (such as our great-great grandparents, or George Washington's toothbrush).

Lastly, we mortals think that questions of whether a particular thing exists or not is settled by experience. Just because we can imagine a volcano in the middle of New York City, it does not follow that there is one. We learn that there is (or is not) such a thing by experience, by employing our senses, by making inferences from what we observe of this world. Ultimately, observation shows us what there is.

That constellation of ideas Parmenides thinks of as the third way, and he thinks it absurd.

PARMENIDES' CRITICISM OF OUR WAY OF THOUGHT

That goddess who is supposedly instructing Parmenides says she wants to "hold him back from that way" on which "mortals" travel. What is that route?

We humans, we mortals, regard the existence of things within a framework in which the notion of possibility occupies a central position. For the most part, we do not think that things we can conceive of must exist or cannot exist. It is possible for flying elephants to exist, but it is also conceivable that no such creatures exist. Whether or not such things exist is a *contingent* feature of the world, not something that can be settled by reason alone.

Furthermore, of things that do exist, we do not (with perhaps rare exceptions) hold that they must exist. It is quite possible that they might not exist. In fact, at least most things that are, were not in existence at some previous time, and (we hold) a time will come when they will again no longer exist. So too for things that do not exist. Many (at least) could exist; many nonexistents did formerly exist; and others will do so in the future.

That group of beliefs, resting on the concepts of possibility and contingency, Parmenides holds to be wholly absurd. Of that group, the present argument is directed particularly against our idea that it is possible (and in fact happens) that things come into being and pass away. That that is the specific object of attack here, comes out in the other pieces of argument we have not yet examined. He says that we think that "the way of all things turns upon itself"—that is, we think things do come into existence and then turn again and pass on. (Incidentally, Parmenides' way of putting that point, his talk of "turning upon itself," may be an allusion to Heraclitus, who *insisted* on the transience of all things.) Again, notice Parmenides' other criticism: "For this shall never be proved: that things that are not are." He implies that humans believe what cannot be proved, namely, that things that do not exist might nonetheless be.

Parmenides, then, found human thoughts about existence complete nonsense. Why? What convinced him of that? Precisely those conclusions reached in the first phase of the inquiry. He had been persuaded by his analysis of the concepts of existence and necessity that to regard a thing as existing is equivalent to thinking that it must exist. Yet when we mortals say "It is, it exists," we assume, contrary to his analysis, that it is possible for the thing not to be. But if a thing that exists *must* exist, then our ordinary idea that its nonbeing is *possible* must be wholly confused.

So too for the case of nonexistence. We humans think that "It does not exist" is compatible with "But someday it might exist." Yet Parmenides' argument has convinced him that for a thing not to be is identical with the impossibility of its existence. Once again, our human way of thought is illegitimate, because it conflicts with the outcome of Parmenides' investigation into the relation between the modal concepts and the concept of existence.

Parmenides' conclusion is that we cannot intelligibly talk and think as we do about existence. We "go along, both deaf and blind, in a daze, creatures without judgment."

REASON AND THE SENSES

Parmenides has argued that (1) nothing new can come into being, nor can things that exist cease existing, and (2) our everyday ideas to the contrary are mad.

A likely response may be made to those contentions, as Parmenides knew full well: "What a silly thing to say, that birth and death, creation and destruction, are not possible. Just open your eyes and ears. You can see the flowers popping out where there were none, watch the cake come into being when before there had been only ingredients, see the house rising in the vacant lot. Or toss a paper into the fire and watch it be destroyed—see the leaves wither and fall and turn to dust. Questions about existence are settled by the senses, by observing the world around us. And what we observe is things coming into being and things passing away."

Parmenides anticipated that objection, for he knew that one component of our ideas about existence is that existential issues are to be settled by resort to experience and observation. He anticipated the criticism and replied to it at the end of what is now Fragment 7: "So do not take that way of thinking. Do not let your habits, born of long experience, force your thoughts in that direction, to travel with an aimless eye, a droning ear and tongue. Rather judge by your reason the contentious refutation I have spoken."

His reply is, essentially, "Don't reject what I have held just because it conflicts with what your senses tell you. That you trust your senses over my argument is just a matter of habit, with no rational basis. Exercise your reason. You will find that my arguments against coming into being and passing away are impeccable and that therefore the senses must be mistaken in telling us the opposite."

We have already seen how Heraclitus began marking a distinction between the senses and reason and how he also asserted the supremacy of our rational faculties over the senses in determining our knowledge of the world. Parmenides carried that one step further so that the senses become *worthless* for learning anything about how things are. From this point on in the history of philosophy, disputes about the relative value of our sensory faculties and our rational powers in forming a proper understanding and knowledge of things become a recurrent feature of philosophical activity. Philosophers began to worry not only about how the world is but also about how we *know* that is how things are.

PARMENIDES, PHILOSOPHY, AND ARGUMENT

In the passage just quoted, Parmenides admonishes his readers to pay attention to "the contentious refutation I have spoken"—that is, to his arguments. That explicit concern with argumentation is highly characteristic of Parmenides and marks another of his contributions to the practice of philosophy.

Earlier I commented that the intellectual tradition begun by the Milesians was distinguished from the mythologers by being *critical*. Progress was made by one thinker subjecting his predecessors' views to criticism. In that process, argument thus became more and more important.

With Parmenides, that development became fully explicit. Parmenides' writing shows how conscious he was of the role of argument in what he was attempting to do. The proper contrast is with Heraclitus, who had also inherited the critical tradition and who certainly had reasons for saying what he did. Nonetheless, Heraclitus did not feel the need to make his patterns of reasoning explicit, but spoke instead in aphorisms, thus giving the results of his thought but not the justification for them. The difference between Heraclitus and Parmenides in this procedural respect is enormous—and Parmenides, with his concern with argument, became the model for future philosophizing.

Incidentally, notice that although Parmenides supports what he had to say with reasons, he nonetheless put the reasoning in the mouth of an authority, a goddess. The modernity of his rationalism consorts very strangely (to our way of thinking) with the appeal to supernatural revelation.

THE FINAL ELIMINATION

Parmenides began by listing three possible ways to think about the existence of anything. He then argued that one of those formal possibilities, the one practiced by human beings, is absurd and so, strictly speaking, is impossible. He continued the inquiry by examining the remaining two options. He concluded that only one of those two routes is really acceptable. The only permissible way of regarding the existence of any object whatsoever is to think that it does and hence *must* exist. The idea that we can conceive of a nonexistent entity is illegitimate. The relevant passages are found in Fragments 2, 3, and 6:

> The other way of thinking, that it is not and cannot be, is wholly impossible. It is impossible because you cannot know what is not nor can you express it [Fragment 2], for it is the same thing which can be thought and which can be [Fragment 3]. What you can speak of and think of has to be, since it can be while nothing cannot be. Think about that. For that is the first way of thinking from which I hold you back [Fragment 6].

PROVING THAT WHAT CAN BE THOUGHT OF, MUST BE

The heart of Parmenides' elimination of the human way was his contention that to say "It is" entails the necessity of its being and to say "It is not" entails the necessity of its not being. Yet that third route tries to talk of being and of not being as if those logical connections did not hold and so as if all manner of possibilities were open.

The objection to the way of thinking now under consideration is quite different. Nothing here hinges on connections between existential claims and modal concepts. Instead, criticism of this mode of thought rests on objections to saying "It is not," to attempts to deny the existence of a thing.

In the relevant (quoted) passage, Parmenides provides two different lines of argument for rejecting one and adopting the other of the two remaining modes of discourse. Both those lines require some clarification—some guesswork, in fact—as to what he meant. (My guess, my interpretation, is not the usual one; that alternative understanding, which I don't believe the text sustains, relies on the thesis that the meaning of a word is the object it refers to.)

The first proof begins with the words "It is impossible [to think 'It is not and cannot be'] because you cannot know what is not nor can you express it. . . ." That is, we cannot think that something is not. Parmenides means that it is impossible to (intelligibly) *assert* the nonexistence of a thing, to *know* it, to *wish* it—in general, it is *impossible to form any conception of a thing's nonbeing.*

Why not? Fragment 3 provides the argument: ". . . for it is the same thing which can be thought and which can be." What does that mean, as an objection to the possibility of denying an object's existence? In the most plausible interpretation, Parmenides is claiming that the thought of a thing is identical with the thought of it as being. His line of argument would go something as follows.

"Think of something—a horse, say. If you have produced the thought of a horse, have pictured a horse to yourself, you have to admit that you pictured it as being, as existing. (Even if you tried to think of the horse as dead, as, for example, stretched out cold in its stall, and thus as not existing, you have failed. For you have only succeeded in picturing a dead horse, something that *is,* something existing there on the floor of the stall.) If you don't think of the horse as existing, then you think of nothing whatsoever, have pictured nothing, and so have not thought of a horse or anything else. My argument, of course, is not restricted to horses—it will work just as well for *any* object you suggest. Therefore, thinking of anything is necessarily thinking of it as being. Consequently, it is impossible to think of a thing as nonexistent. That way is wholly impossible."

One other line of reasoning is introduced by Parmenides to support his thesis that we cannot meaningfully say that things are not: "What you can speak of and think of has to be, since it can be while nothing cannot be."

How are we to understand that enigmatic argument? The crucial item in it is the word "nothing." Parmenides must be assuming that anything nonexistent is, or would be, nothing at all. Given that, he seems to have fashioned the following argument: "What does not exist would be nothing. So thinking of what is not, would be thinking of nothing. But we cannot think of nothing—if we think, we must think of something. Therefore, it is impossible to think of, conceive of, the nonexistent. Whenever we think of any object, we must think of it as existing. That is, the way we *must* think is *that it is*—we cannot say 'It is not.' "

ASSESSING THE PROOFS

Rejection of the third way, the human way, ultimately rested on Parmenides' analysis of the logical relationship between existence claims and the modal concepts. Rejection of the second way, and therewith "proof" of the first as the only intelligible way to think, has a different foundation, although that too has to do with conceptual, logical connections. Only this time the concepts in question are those of *thought* and *existence*.

Those proofs of Parmenides need critical scrutiny. For the first of them to work, his assumption that to think of something is to picture it to oneself, to form a mental image of it, must be acceptable. Yet that assumption is very questionable. For the second argument to succeed, Parmenides' assumption that the nonexistent is nothing and that therefore to think of what is not is to think of nothing must be correct. Again, that assumption has serious problems. Moreover, probably neither proof will even be initially plausible in connection with the other (as yet unexamined) senses of "is."

"IT IS AND IT MUST BE"

The outcome of the first half of the Way of Truth is that "*it is and it must be.*" That is, Parmenides takes himself to have established that each and every possible object of thought and speech is, exists, and that it must exist.

Obviously, this is a most astonishing conclusion. The world is vastly different from what we think it to be—it lacks nothing, in fact. Furthermore, there is no contingency about such matters of existence, no possibility of its being otherwise, no point to exploring the world to learn what there is. Thought is quite enough to settle the issue—and it is always settled one way, namely, that the thing exists.

APPLYING PARMENIDES' VIEWS
TO THE PREDICATIVE "IS"

Up to here, the account of Parmenides' position and of his arguments in defense of that position have been worked out in terms of a particular interpretation of "is." The formulas "It is" and "It is not" have been taken to mean "It exists" and "It does not exist." However, Parmenides was not concerned only with the existential use of "is." The second, *predicative*, use of "is"—as in "is fat," "is grumpy," "is on top of"—was of equal interest. In fact, everything so far claimed about Parmenides on the topic of the "is" of existence must be applied (with appropriate minor modifications) to this second use of the word. Here, in summary form, is that application:

1. Any object that can be thought of can be thought to have or to not have any of a quite large range of properties and relations. (I say "quite large," because not every property or relation can be assigned to or denied of every thing: "is having trouble breathing" and "is to the left of the barn" can be said of or denied of horses, for example, but not of the number 2 or of a sneeze or of the U.S. Constitution.) We can also think of or say of a thing that we do not know whether it has a given attribute, that we have no idea whether it stands in a certain relation or not.

2. Parmenides' most important theses about predication are analogs of his central claims about existence: (a) if something has a certain property (or relation), it must have it; and (b) if a thing lacks a given characteristic, it could not have it. If we can say "It is pink," we must mean "It has to be pink." Similarly, Parmenides held that "He is not smiling" means the same as "He could not be smiling."

His reasons for those contentions must also have been analogs of his arguments concerning existence. If we can say "It is pink," we must mean "It has to be pink," for if a pink thing does not have to be pink, it could be other than pink; yet being pink and also being other than pink is contradictory and thus impossible. Similarly, since "is not smiling" is incompatible with "is smiling," it follows (Parmenides held) that whatever is not smiling cannot be otherwise. Being otherwise (smiling) would mean that a nonsmiling thing might be smiling, but it is impossible to be both.

In general, "It is not" ("fat, taller than," and so on) "and it cannot be so" is one way of thought and speech. A second is "It is" ("wise, more intelligent than," and so on) "and it must be that way."

3. Mortals think and speak as if there were yet another intelligible route regarding predication. We take it to be *possible* for an object that is a given way not to be that way. If Johnny is here (is clean, is bigger than, and so forth), we do not think it *necessary* that he be here, and so forth. We think that it is a *contingent* fact—just the way the world happens to be—that he is here. He might well have been and might well later be elsewhere. In short, we, in our normal patterns of thought, think of the features and relationships of objects (at least most such properties) as subject to change, as possibly (even probably) coming to be different from what they are at any given time. Moreover, we also think that the way to discover in what condition a thing is, is by *experience*, by exploring it, by employing our sensory faculties in making discoveries about it.

4. But, says Parmenides, those common views of human beings are wildly mistaken, even nonsense. There is no sense to that talk of contingency, to that belief in the possibility of change, in connection with the properties possessed by a thing. To be one way (sober, lazy, and so on) is to have to be that way—to not be this or that (fat, in love with, and so on) means that it is impossible to be this or that. The truth of those contentions, and hence the wrongheadedness of the human way of thought, is established by the arguments in Item 2.

5. To any protest that we can see, smell, hear (and so on) changes in the properties and relations of objects, Parmenides replies that such a claim only shows our senses cannot be trusted to discover the truth. The preceding arguments refute what experience seems to reveal. To opt for experience in the face of those unanswered arguments is to choose what is merely habitual over what rationality shows to be the truth.

6. There are thus only two ways to regard the possession of properties: either a thing is P and must be P, or it is not P and cannot be so. However, the second way also turns out to be impossible, on further critical scrutiny. That is, Parmenides also fashions arguments aimed at showing that it is impossible to form a conception of a thing's not being P.

It is very difficult to plausibly represent how Parmenides argues for that thesis. His actual arguments on this subject, at least as most reasonably interpreted, work much better for the "is" of existence than for the "is" of predication. Since he did not have available this distinction between the two senses of the word, he almost certainly framed his arguments very generally—in terms of a sweeping "It is" and "It is not"—and thus was not in a position to notice how awkwardly they fit the case of "It is P" and "It is not P." To think of something may seem to require thinking of it (picturing it) as being—but thinking of something does not seem to necessitate thinking of it (picturing it) as, for example, red or fat or victorious. Again, to think of what is not as nothing, may seem plausible when the "is" is not specified more precisely. But to contend that to think of what does not have the property P (red or cute or hairy) as being nothing or having nothing by way of properties is not at all convincing.

7. Despite the inadequacies of his arguments as applied to predication, Parmenides concludes that we cannot think of a thing as not having a given property. We cannot sensibly say "It is not this way"—the only way we can properly think is that a thing is such-and-such and must be such-and-such.

INCLUDING IDENTITY IN THE SCOPE OF PARMENIDES' THESES

Recall the third sense of "is" to which the Parmenidean machinery was applied: we use "is" to say that something identified in one way also bears a second identity, as in "Joe DiMaggio was the Yankee Clipper." Having just reviewed how Parmenides' theses are to be applied to predication, I shall be very brief concerning the application to identity.

There is no possibility, Parmenides held, of acquiring or losing identities. For *any* object, if it is the president of the United States, then it must be, or, if it is not, then it cannot be. And that will hold over the entire range of names and descriptions. Moreover, it is impossible to think or say that two things are not the same—we cannot meaningfully say, for example, "That" (pointing to or designating *anything whatsoever*) "is not my wife."

SUMMARY

It is time to draw the threads of the discussion in this chapter together. Parmenides has argued that the following holds true of any object we can think of. We cannot say or think that any thing does not exist, that it does not have some property or feature or stand in some relation, that it is not the same as something else. Nor can we say or think of anything that it might not exist or might not have some characteristic or might lack a certain identity—nor can it be said that it might at one time not have been that way or might at some future time come not to be that way.

All that can be said is "It is and must be."

8

PARMENIDES II: CONSEQUENCES

Earlier I said that the Way of Truth consists of two projects. Parmenides' first aim was to establish a basic principle, and then to show its consequences. We have now worked our way through that initial project. He argued that the only intelligible answer to the question "Is it?"—where the "it" is taken to range over any conceivable object and where the "is" is understood in any sense—is "It must be." It is now time to see what consequences are to be derived from that answer.

CONSEQUENCE: THERE CANNOT BE CHANGE

The first, and most obvious, outcome is that there can be no change. To think of a thing as something that can change, it *must* make sense to think of it as being (this) and then as not being (this). That is what change is. Yet, in rejecting the human way of thought as absurd for each of the three readings of "is," Parmenides has held that such possibilities, such ways of speaking and thinking, do not make sense. What is has to be and cannot be otherwise.

Suppose we now assume, as it seems likely that Parmenides did, that everything that can be said of a thing can be formulated in terms of one or the other of the three forms of "is." It then follows that there is no respect in which an object can possibly be other than it is. If it cannot be other than it is, it cannot change, cannot alter its existential status, its properties and relations, its identities.

Lastly, if no changes can occur in anything, then there aren't any. Despite what our senses and our experience seem to reveal, nothing changes.

That denial of the possibility of change, that presentation of the world as static, as always the same, has long been recognized to be a major feature of Parmenides' thought. Coming as he does immediately after Heraclitus in the historical succession, the denial of change has seemed all the more striking. For the central thesis of Heraclitus had been that change is the fundamental category of the universe: stability is an illusion, change is unchanging. How swiftly, people have thought, that view provoked its opposite!

The implicit causal claim is misguided. It is doubtful that Heraclitus' views *provoked* Parmenides into thinking the opposite. The sources of Parmenides' denial of change can be described without any interesting references to Heraclitus. Parmenides was opposing a common human idea about change, an idea that Heraclitus had carried to an extreme.

More than that, it is important to notice one way in which Parmenides was not in conflict with Heraclitus at all. Parmenides need not deny that Heraclitus was correct *if* the Heraclitean view is restricted to what we *observe*, to the world we experience. Nothing in Parmenides' position requires him to deny that the basic feature of the "world" we learn of through our senses is in a state of unceasing change. Parmenides *does* contend that that is not what *really* happens. What really happens is nothing. Heraclitus' mistake, from the Parmenidean point of view, is that he took what we learn via the senses to be relevant to any account of reality.

Plato will later exploit the possibility that Heraclitus and Parmenides need not be in conflict over change. Plato will be Heraclitean about the objects of our senses and hold that they are perpetually changing—and he will also be Parmenidean and deny that our senses reveal reality. Moreover, for Plato, reality is discovered by reason, and as for Parmenides, no change is to be found "there"; that is, what is real does not change.

CONSEQUENCE: THE FURNITURE OF THE WORLD CONSISTS OF JUST ONE PIECE

Parmenides argued that whatever can be thought of must exist. On the basis of that argument, we might think he would have thought that the world is an incredibly rich place, packed with every conceivable object. That is not, however, his ultimate conclusion about the constituents of reality. To hold that there are very many things in existence is to hold that each one *is not the same as* the others. To say that there are two things, Sam and Janet, is to assume that Sam is not Janet. But according to the identity interpretation of the argument regarding "is," it is impossible to say "This is not the same as that." All that can be said or thought is "This is the same as that." Hence, Sam must be the same as Janet. Repeated applications of that principle show that it is *impossible that there could be more than one thing*. All names and identifying phrases are names and descriptions of one and the same thing. *It* is and must be.

His arguments yield the conclusion that there is only one thing—the One, as it came to be called. What needs to be understood clearly is the nature of Parmenides' monism.

With the exception of the Pythagoreans, the Pre-Socratics before Parmenides were monists. On the whole, they subscribed to the view that one underlying form of stuff makes up the many things of which the world is composed. Heraclitus went even further in holding the world to be a unity—even such "abstract" entities as war and peace are one (thing), are secretly connected into an intelligible system that Heraclitus thinks of as making them one.

Notice that all those predecessors of Parmenides take it that *there are many items* in the world that have an underlying connection, that are in the specified ways the same. And their arguments for that position are (excluding Heraclitus to some degree) *cosmological*—they are monists because they believe in only one stuff, out of which the developed world has evolved.

Parmenides' monism rejects the idea that the world is composed of many things with an underlying identity of stuff. There is only one thing. Furthermore, his reasons for that thesis are not cosmological, not scientific—he did not assume that you could account for the ways of the world by postulating one kind of stuff. Rather, his reasons for holding to a monism are based on *logic*, on what we *must mean* when we say "It is" and "It is not," and the consequences of having to mean that.

So, although outwardly Parmenides takes his place with his predecessors as a monist, the doctrine as he developed it involved something radically new and radically different from what had come before. To put it bluntly (and for now possibly obscurely), their monism was physical, his was metaphysical.

CONSEQUENCE: "WHAT IS" IS INDESCRIBABLE

In connection with the predicative use of "is," we saw that Parmenides' arguments produce the claim that it is impossible to deny that a thing possesses a given property. All that can sensibly be said is that it has this property and must have it. That conclusion makes it appear that a thing has every conceivable property and stands in every conceivable relationship. The One, it seems, must be *both* fat and skinny, red and white and green, heavier and lighter than, and so on and on. Is that state of affairs not contradictory? And has not Parmenides rejected views on the ground that they lead to contradictions?

That is how things look, but once again we must keep in mind the subtlety of Parmenides' position. First of all, given that there is only the One, all relational predicates vanish from any account of reality. That is because any relation, such as "John is taller than Mary," involves *two* things standing in a certain relation. But, the argument goes, more than one thing cannot exist. No relational predicate can be applied in a world composed of but one item. The One has no relations because there is nothing for it to be related to.

More broadly, to think that things might have more than one property (or relation) presumes that each property is not the same as another. "It is red" and "It is blue" seem contradictory because it is assumed that red *is not* (the same color as) blue. However, Parmenides has argued that it makes no sense to say "is not the same as." In consequence, the only truth is red is blue is fat is taller than is. . . . Property words all come to the same thing.

It is not completely clear how to continue from here. With names and identifying phrases, it was simple enough to suggest that since they did not, could not, name different things, they must name the same thing. It is difficult to make that move with predicates. Are we to think that there is only one property *It* has? It is probably best to conclude that "what is"—the One—is *characterless, featureless*. Property ascriptions would make sense only if they could mark out different features. However, it is unintelligible to use the language of predicates to mark out differences. Hence the idea that "what is" has any features is unintelligible. Lastly, if the One *did* have a property, it would make sense to think that it is not the same as its property. But that denial of sameness, that assertion of difference, is impossible.

Consequently, "what is" is featureless, is indescribable. *All* that can be said is "It exists" and "It is the same as itself."

REALITY AND APPEARANCE

The account of the immediate consequences of Parmenides' arguments is not complete. One or two points of general concern remain for us to reflect on. Earlier in the text, I pointed out that Parmenides was explicitly drawing a distinction between the senses and reason and was maintaining that the senses are worthless as guides to the truth. In the preceding discussion (of the consequences of holding that all that can be thought is "It is and must be"), I relied on another related distinction between *appearance* and *reality*. This distinction, too, becomes explicit with Parmenides.

Philosophers, of course, did not invent that distinction; it is a feature of human language to distinguish between how things seem, appear, look, and so on, and how they (really) are; for example, "It looks like her, but it can't be." So though not inventing them, philosophers before Parmenides had employed those distinctions in telling their philosophical and scientific stories. There seem to be many things, they suggested, yet they are all (for example) really forms of water, and so on. The resort to the distinctions between appearance and reality was vital to Heraclitus: things appear stable but they really are not. It was but a short step from there to Parmenides, who finds a major role for the distinction in his own system.

Parmenides also hooked the two distinctions—between reason and the senses, and between reality and appearance—together. Reason alone is capable of apprehending how things (really) are, while the senses are good only for learning how things seem to be. Combining those two distinctions is most certainly a philosophical step, for we do not ordinarily make that arrangement: it may, for example, *look* like her coming through the fog, yet to find out we *look* once again. And we certainly do reason about what we observe. Parmenides' philosophical move in making those connections has deeply influenced philosophy down through the centuries.

METAPHYSICS

At a couple of places, I have claimed that Parmenides was a metaphysician, the first metaphysician, and contrasted him with his predecessors (except for

Heraclitus, to some extent) by characterizing them as physicists. It is now time to produce some clarification of those claims.

A scientist, even such early ones as the Milesians, postulates, infers, some hidden reality to explain certain patterns in what we observe of the world. That is, scientific theories aim at making sense of what we learn about the world through our experience of it. Heraclitus, for example, posited processes of small but unceasing change, and he inferred those changes in order to account for the larger changes that a thing (such as a person's face or a stone) reveals over a longer period of time. Modern scientists inferred the existence of atoms to explain the patterns of behavior of substances.

That was not Parmenides' game. What he inferred reality to be, and to be *like,* does not help to make any sense of the things we observe. Parmenidean reality does not account for any feature of observation. In fact, to hold that reality consists of an unchangeable One is to make what our senses show us problematic rather than intelligible.

That imperviousness to facts of experience is characteristic of metaphysical theories. Furthermore, those theories have their origin in *logic,* not in what we have learned from experience. Parmenides, like other metaphysicians, begins with *what it means to say* such-and-such (in his case with what it means to talk about necessity, impossibility, and possibility). From answers to those questions about what such-and-such means, it seems that the philosopher can see how the world must ultimately be, quite independently of how it ordinarily seems to be. The game is metaphysics, not science.

CONSEQUENCES FOR SCIENCE

We possess one very long fragment, Fragment 8, which begins, "There is but one way left to be spoken of, that it is." In the nearly fifty lines following, Parmenides is obviously drawing (at some length) conclusions concerning "what is."

Although specifying the consequences of the thesis that the only conceivable thought is "It is," I made no textual references. I did not, that is, point out where in the text Parmenides said that such-and-such follows from his thesis. I merely said them to be consequences and claimed that Parmenides recognized them to be such.

The interpretative problem is that although all those consequences are either implicit in or presupposed by Fragment 8, when Parmenides comes to cite what follows from his central line of argument, he seems to be doing *more* than what I have already noted. There seems to be some further shift in his thinking. Montgomery Furth, in an important paper on Parmenides, says of the material in Fragment 8, "I regard the cosmological conclusions of the 'The Way of Truth' . . . as remote corollaries of principles of a purely logical kind whose working is the real point of the poem" (1974, p. 249).

In Furth's terms, Fragment 8 represents a shift from a purely logical concern to a cosmological, scientific concern on Parmenides' part. That strikes me as nearly right. What I suspect that Parmenides does is to introduce an *assumption* that governs the manner in which he draws his conclusions. He sees that the metaphysical corollaries of his principles are (1) that there cannot be more than one thing, (2) that the idea of properties makes no sense, and (3) that change is impossible. Now, in speaking further of what is, he assumes that It is a *thing*, a hunk of stuff, composed of matter, a spatial object.

In short, Fragment 8 contains the consequences of his logical-metaphysical theses as applied to what is, *where* what is is conceived of as a material entity. He is trying to make clear the bearing of his conceptual analyses on the scientific tradition. The consequences (for cosmology and science) of his doctrine need to be discussed.

Science and Change
Parmenides' argument against the possibility of change ran thus:

> *Premise:* For change to be possible, both "it is" and "it is not" would have to make sense.
>
> *Premise:* But "it is not" is unintelligible.
>
> *Conclusion:* Hence, it is not possible for *It* to be other than it is.

That conclusion is taken to be a matter of logic, of reason.

In Fragment 8, the most extended application of the logical doctrines is to the issue of cosmic change. Parmenides is intent on pointing out to the cosmological and scientific tradition that given his previous reasoning, there can be no such thing as coming to be and passing away. He begins by saying that "what is, is unborn and imperishable" and concludes, twenty-one lines later, "Thus coming into being is extinguished and perishing is unimaginable."

In between those two quotes, he attempts to show that that is so. Although some of his moves there are of interest as semi-independent objections to the generation of "what is," what he says is largely a variation on, or a spelling out of, the conclusion previously reached: "On this topic, the decision lies here: It is or it is not. And that decision has already been made."

Still, one point about that application needs to be made. Although he bills his argument as showing that both coming to be and passing away are impossible, when you look at what he actually says there, he only discusses coming to be. Why did he not find it necessary to argue against perishing? There seem to be two answers. First, it may be easier to see that perishing requires a transition from "It is" to "It is not" than it is to notice that coming into being requires a transition from "It is not" to "It is." Parmenides wanted to make very sure that that was not missed. Yet (second) another reason, something specific about the scientific tradition, seems to have led him to emphasize the absence of creation while merely mentioning the impossibility of destruction. Mourelatos (see Bibliography at the end of the chapter) puts it best:

We should recall in this connection that the idea of basic realities which were "deathless" was part of an old and familiar conception of the world. It was no doubt part of the Milesian world-view; and it was an outgrowth of the Homeric and Hesiodic conception of gods and divine powers. Nevertheless in the Milesian as much as in the Homeric scheme, one had the option of inquiring into the *origin* of these basic realities. For Parmenides, a sustained *logos,* "rational account," will disclose that "generation" is no more possible than "perishing" for what is. . . . As a doctrine, this extension of the attribute of permanence to encompass nongeneration is not wholly new: Heraclitus had said of cosmic fire that "it was, is and will be, " and one may assume that Anaximander would have spoken of the *apeiron,* the "boundless," in similar terms. In Parmenides we get an argument for this symmetrical denial of birth and death. (1970, p. 97)

If coming into being is impossible, then cosmogony is equally impossible. There is no story to be told about the origin of the cosmos. Moreover, as the denial of coming into being and perishing encompasses not just the existence of things, but also of properties, relations, and so on, it certainly looks as if science as a whole becomes impossible. There are no natural processes to be studied. Hence science, which had such a promising start with the Milesians, now looks as if it were a wholly misguided enterprise with nowhere to go.

Religion and Change

The tendency of Pre-Socratic thought prior to Parmenides had been to reject, at least in theory, the culturally given gods and to replace them with a god discovered in the process of inquiry. Because the stuff of the cosmos was said to be imperishable and because that same thing was taken to be capable of self-transformation in a rational, orderly fashion, it was thought that that out of which the world sprang was a worthy divine being.

Parmenides' conclusions do not fit in with that developing religious conception. If the world is incapable of activity and is without any qualities or features, how, despite its imperishability, can it be looked on as an object of religious veneration? It is simply a hunk of unchanging stuff about which the question of rationality does not arise.

Not only does "what is," the One, not lend itself to a religious interpretation, but there is no evidence in the poem that Parmenides deeply regretted that absence. Despite his having come from a Pythagorean background, nothing indicates that the mature Parmenides had those spiritual longings characteristic of the Pythagoreans or the Italian branch of Greek philosophy. (One might say jokingly that Parmenides claimed a greater unity between humans and the universe than Pythagoras ever dreamed of.)

The Timelessness of "What Is"

Both in our ordinary dealings with the world and its objects and in those specialized investigations of that world we call "science," the concepts of space and time are absolutely central to our understanding. Parmenides, when noting the consequences of his logical theses on scientific investigation, had occasion to discuss their relevance for both space and time. Let us begin with the latter.

According to Parmenides, all that can be said intelligibly is "It is and it must be." And he notes that, consequently, "what is" must be uncreated and imperishable. It thus looks as if we could reason, "Since It *is* and since It did not come into being and It cannot pass away, therefore It has always been and will always be." By that line of reasoning, "what is" is located in time and has unlimited temporal duration—is everlasting.

Such a view would not be striking among the Pre-Socratics. Anaximander most likely thought of the *apeiron* as being around forever. Heraclitus said as much of his *arché*, the principle of things, fire: "The order which is common to all was not made by god or man, but it forever was, is and will be; an ever-lasting fire" (Fragment 30).

Yet that interpretation of Parmenides depends on taking the "is" in "It is" to be in the present tense and then inferring that It has persisted through all past time and will do so through all future time. But not all occurrences of the word "is" are present tense. Especially in mathematics, the use of "is" is *tenseless*. "A triangle is a three-sided figure" does not admit of such questions as "When did it become that way?" and "How long will it be that way?" About mathematical objects, it makes no sense to talk about the past and the future. If "was" (past tense) and "will be" (future) do not make sense in mathematical propositions, the mathematical "is" cannot be in the present tense: for "present" only makes sense by way of contrast to a past and a future tense. Thus the verb in "2 + 3 is 5," and so on, is tenseless.

That situation is usually marked by saying that logical and mathematical propositions are *eternal* truths. It is also usual to infer that mathematical objects, such as the circle, the number 2, are *eternal objects*—that is, they are outside of time, are not temporal entities. As such they are to be contrasted with *everlasting objects,* objects in time, that have a temporal duration, but that exist forever, through all time.

Parmenides said, "Nor was it at any time, nor will it be; for it is now, all together, one and continuous" (Fragment 9, line 5). That sentence certainly looks as if he were denying that we can say of "what is" that "It was and it will be." If he did deny that, then he meant that "It is" is tenseless, is an eternal truth. Moreover, he probably inferred from the eternity of the truth "It is" that "what is" is eternal—that It is a timeless object and not (like Heraclitus' cosmic fire) something that exists forever.

Scholars have doubted that Parmenides did hold that "what is" is timeless and so that he saw the distinction between everlasting and eternal. He certainly does not always avoid temporal language in speaking of "what is"— in fact, in the preceding assertion where he presumably denies that It has a past or a future, he goes on to say, "for it is now. . . ." "Now" is a time word, referring to the present. Hence Parmenides manages to talk of time immediately after seemingly canceling it.

Despite such awkward occurrences and the doubts they raise, most likely Parmenides aimed to hold that "what is" is outside of time. His lapses into temporal language can be reasonably explained away (though not always *easily*).

So far, I have said that Parmenides made a distinction between time and eternity and held that "what is" is timeless. But why did he say that? What were his reasons? There is no definite answer in the text. The claim that *It* is timeless occurs as the final item in a list of assertions concerning "what is" and is followed by arguments concerning the first item on that list, namely that *It* does not change. The usual assumption is that Parmenides thought that timelessness follows from the absence of change. If that led him to his view, not until Aristotle did it become clear *how* the absence of change could be held to be incompatible with the passage of time. Between Parmenides and Aristotle, with Plato as the major figure, an extended inquiry was made into the nature of time. Parmenides can be credited with initiating that inquiry and consequently with having shown *time* to be a philosophical problem.

Space: Full and Empty

Although he banished time from reality to appearance, Parmenides did not do the same for space. It certainly looks as if his general line of argument would have entitled him to do so. Spatial expressions such as "A is to the left of B," "A is larger than B," "A is at coordinates X, Y, Z," and "A is here" should be as senseless as any other relational and predicative statement. But in fact Parmenides seems not at all tempted to notice those possibilities. He assumes that "what is" is in space, that It can take spatial characterizations. That is probably because he comes to think of "what is" as a stuff, and a stuff is in space.

Although he does not raise questions about the existence of space, he does have important things to say about it. The scientific tradition had assumed that areas of space could have more or less of the stuff of the world in them, possibly even none. The notion of empty space, a void, was important to the Pythagoreans. In representing numbers spatially—the number 3 is . · .—for that representation to differ from 1(· . ·), empty space, a void, must exist between the units. Or consider Anaximenes. If air is capable of rarefying and condensing, then empty space must exist as well as air, so that the air can be compressed or expanded.

Parmenides denies the possibility of empty space and with it any sort of activity in connection with "what is" that requires a void: "Nor is it divisible, since it is all alike. There is not more of it in one place than another, which would prevent its coherence—all is full of what is. It is thus continuous as what is coheres to what is" (Fragment 8, lines 22–25).

Why is there no void, no empty space? Precisely because he thinks of "what is" as a stuff. If "what is" is matter, then empty space would be a place where "what is" is not. What could that be but what is not? And the impossibility of not being has already been established. Hence, since not being is impossible and empty space would be not being, there cannot be a void. So "all is full of what is." Consequently, since "it is all alike"—that is, it is not a combination of stuff and empty space—it is impossible to divide it; cutting something in half requires creating a space between the two parts. Nor can there be such natural processes as thickening and thinning, having "more of it in one place than another"—for those processes require empty space.

As with time, problems about space, full and empty, become significant issues for science and philosophy after, and in consequence of, Parmenides. One point must be kept in mind when we pass on to later developments: Parmenides' argument for the impossibility of empty space was not a strict consequence of the arguments in the first half of the Way of Truth. Rather, his denial that there can be empty space hinged on an assumption quite independent of arguments alleging that we cannot say "It is not." He assumes that "what is" is a stuff. Empty space is thought to be "what is not," not-being, only because he presumes that "what is" must be material, something in space. Later criticism will focus on that assumption.

The Immovability of "What Is"

It is very certain that Parmenides holds that "what is" does not move. "Motionless, limited by mighty bonds . . . remaining the same and in the same place, it is by itself, staying firmly where it is (Fragment 8, lines 26–30). What is less certain is the precise point, at this place in the text, of his insistence on the absence of motion.

One thing is clear: Parmenides' theses about being and not-being have as a consequence the impossibility of a thing moving from one place to another. For if it (whatever) is *here,* then it cannot *not* be *here,* and so it cannot be *there*—which is what a change of place would require. Change is impossible, and motion is just one type of change.

In all likelihood, that is part of what Parmenides meant to point out here—"what is" does not move because the idea of change of position is senseless. (A few lines later he explicitly says that "change of place" is nothing more than a name invented by mortals.) Nonetheless, if the line of argument concerned with the impossibility of not-being is pushed hard, the distinction between "here" and "there"—that is, "not-here"—turns out to be senseless, and with that the entire idea of space is threatened. Yet, as we have seen, Parmenides firmly locates "what is" in space. So perhaps we should look elsewhere for what he is up to when he asserts the immobility of what is.

There is a second reason, then, behind Parmenides' denial of motion, one appropriate to his present concern with his cosmologically minded predecessors. He has just denied that there could be empty space, has asserted that all is full of "what is." If so, if all places are filled, there is no place for "what is" to move into. There is no other vacant place into which it could move.

The trouble with that line of argument is that it leaves rotational movement—spinning as a top does—possible. And yet Parmenides denied all motion. Did he miss seeing that rotational motion escapes this line of reasoning?

"What Is" Is Limited and Complete

When Parmenides said, "Motionless, limited by mighty bonds . . ." (Fragment 8, line 26), we should be interested not only in the reference to the immobility of "what is," but also in the idea that "what is" is limited. In these final lines of the fragment, the ideas of *limitation* and *completeness* recur frequently. He says that It stays firmly where It is, "For powerful Necessity restrains and limits it on every side, because, according to law, what is cannot be incomplete; for what is cannot need something further . . ." (Fragment 8, lines 31–33). Again (lines 42–44), "However, since there is an outer limit, it is completed: just as a ball is well-rounded, evenly developed in every direction from the center."

Parmenides talks as if being complete were equivalent to being limited. He seems to argue, "If 'what is' were unlimited, it would be unfinished, incomplete, not a perfect whole; but reality cannot be incomplete since that would require something else to complete it and there cannot be anything other than what is; hence reality must be complete and hence limited."

The word translated "limited" here is an old acquaintance, namely *peras*. Thus, Parmenides is arguing that "what is" is not *apeiron* and so may be objecting to Anaximander. Remember too that the Pythagoreans conceived the universe to be composed ultimately of two basic principles, the limited and the unlimited. Parmenides is rejecting that idea also—there is no such thing as the unlimited. To see that he retains only one of the Pythagorean principles is one way of understanding his monism. In fact, consulting the Pythagorean list of opposites shows that all Parmenides' assertions about the nature of "what is" mention items to be found only on the side of limitation: it is one, at rest, straight (equally extended from the middle), good (complete).

Sphericity

When Parmenides urges the completeness of "what is," he goes on to say "just as a ball is well-rounded, evenly developed in every direction from the center." This line has sparked a good deal of controversy. Did Parmenides mean that reality is spherical, or is the reference to be taken metaphorically? The issue here really concerns the reading of the entire eighth fragment in which Parmenides is drawing consequences and has to do with whether he there conceives of "what is" as a kind of stuff extended in space. I have long since adopted that interpretation and so now am committed to saying that Parmenides did hold that reality is spherical.

The idea that the universe is round became deeply embedded in Greek thought and far beyond that in the history of astronomy and the entire history of Western civilization.

THE WAY OF SEEMING

Having been given a most lengthy tour of the Way of Truth, the reader may be shocked to be reminded that what we have covered in that extensive discussion is only the first half (or so) of the poem. On recalling the existence of another major segment of Parmenides' poem and now having learned what Parmenides said about "what is," we could find it difficult to understand what more he could have talked about.

Most surprising of all, when we look at those extant fragments of what is called the Way of Seeming (or Appearance), we clearly see that Parmenides was producing a *cosmological system.* Yet we must ask how he *could* have had *that* as a project when the Way of Truth argued, in effect, that nothing cosmologically (scientifically) can be said about the world. No other interpretative problem about Parmenides has caused more difficulty than the question "Why was he engaging in cosmological speculation when his metaphysics and logic (seemingly) rendered such an activity unintelligible?"

Evidence in the fragments bears on his aims in producing a cosmological system in the second half of the poem. In the Prologue, the unnamed goddess who, technically, has been talking throughout the Way of Truth, told Parmenides that she would teach him not only the truth but also "how things seem to mortals, in which there is no truth. Despite that lack of truth, you must learn how what seems to be must be because it is accepted." (Serious difficulties afflict the translation of that last sentence—my version is only approximate.) We also possess the lines in which she makes the transition from the first lesson, concerning truth, to the second: "Here I end the trustworthy account, the thought which concerns the truth. Now you are to learn how things seem to mortals, noting well the deceit in the pattern of my words" (Fragment 8, lines 50–52).

The goddess is thus quite clear that the story of the cosmos that she will now relate to Parmenides is *not the truth.* Truth is to be found only in the earlier account. Rather, the cosmological story she will tell has to do with the opinions and experience of mortals, what the world is like to them.

In truth, there *is* no differentiated universe that undergoes change—but it *seems* to us humans that there is. Moreover, Parmenides must have thought that it is possible to produce an account of the development and nature of what appears to us to be true. Perhaps the best model for understanding Parmenides' enterprise here is to compare the world humans experience to a dream or a complete hallucination. What we dream is not what is really happening at the time (we dream we are flying when, in fact, we are asleep in bed). Yet, our dreams are typically not complete chaos—no matter how untrue they are and no matter how disorganized, we can discover patterns or regularities in them. If Parmenides conceived our experience of the world to be like a dream, then we can understand why he thought he could engage in thought about the details of that experience—although, strictly speaking, such events and things as occur in our experience are not-being. (Plato later improved on that scheme by allowing not only for being and non-being, but also for a third, intermediate, class he called "becoming," which included what Parmenides took to be involved in our experienced world.)

Why should he *want* to do that, want to tell a cosmological tale that cannot be the truth about how things are? The goddess says to him (Fragment 8, lines 60–61), "The entire arrangement I will tell you as is most likely, so that no ideas of mortals will outdo you." She certainly seems to be saying that it is possible to tell better and worse stories about appearances and that she will teach him the best possible stories so that no other human shall produce a better cosmology.

The Extent of His Scheme

We do not have many fragments concerned with the details of Parmenides' cosmological scheme. But from what is available and from ancient testimony, what he attempted was certainly ambitious. His aim seems to have been to work out both the history and the present arrangement of the world of human experience with a breadth comparable to that of Anaximander's cosmic system—a project befitting one whose intent was to produce an account of how things appear that could not be outdone by others.

His system included a cosmogony that related the development of the cosmos from its origin down through the origin of humanity and other animals. He included a theogony in his history of the universe. As typical with the Pre-Socratic cosmologists, his discussion of heavenly phenomena was fairly thorough, astronomy being the most advanced scientific study in the ancient world. One special topic was a theory of perception and sensation, including comments on perceptual knowledge.

A Dualistic World

Although much of the detailed cosmology has vanished, ancient commentators did manage to preserve the general principles of his cosmic construction. Quite important in that connection is that fact that he explicitly rejected monistic accounts. He described how the world seems to mortals in terms of *two* ultimate *arché*, or principles. Thus, though reality was, for Parmenides, a unity, the world we think real has two constituents. In fact, monism in Greek cosmology was largely put to rest by Parmenides. The systems that followed him were pluralistic.

The two principles at the root of the varied and variable perceptual world were called by Parmenides light and night. But those were not their only designations: he also referred to light as fire and no doubt thought of it as the hot. Night, or darkness, was presumably earth, the cold. As so common in those Greek systems, the primary cosmic constituents were thought to be opposites.

But unlike the Milesian schemes, these opposites were fundamental, neither derived from anything else nor one from another. When Parmenides said, speaking of those two forms, that "one must not name one only" (Fragment 8, line 54), he may have been urging that a differentiated universe cannot be derived from only a single ultimate principle; that a sensible cosmology must be, at least, dualistic. Furthermore, he clearly insists that those two *arché* are each wholly self-identical and so not reducible to each other. In Fragment 9 he calls them "both equal," and in Fragment 8 he says that fire is "everywhere the same as itself but not the same as the other." Neither is reducible to the other, neither is merely a variant of the other.

In holding that, Parmenides appears not only to have originated the idea that the standard cosmic stuffs, fire and earth, cannot be transmuted into each other, but he also seems to have produced a conception of how they interacted that bore fruit in later cosmologies: ". . . all things are full of Light and of obscure Night" (Fragment 9). The idea seems to be that all the objects of the perceived world are composed of some of each of the two basic stuffs. This idea of things as mixtures was thoroughly developed by Parmenides' successors.

Parmenides' Pythagoreanism

Parmenides was reputed to have been a Pythagorean as a young man, and his dualistic cosmology most clearly shows the remains of his intellectual upbringing. There are differences, of course. For instance, Parmenides does not mathematize the universe. Whereas the Pythagoreans tended to think of their two ultimate principles as two very different sorts of things, the unlimited as a stuff into which the limited as a *formal* principle was inserted to produce order, Parmenides appears rather to regard light and night as both stuffs. And certainly the main difference is that Parmenides denied that the cosmological system had any genuine truth to it. Yet there are correspondences between the Pythagorean dualism and that of Parmenides.

One possible Pythagorean hangover in Parmenides' cosmology concerns the extent to which Parmenides thought one of the two ultimate principles was of more moral worth than the other. Recall that on the Pythagorean list of opposites, "good" was included under the heading of the limited, "bad" under the unlimited column. Some indications show that Parmenides thought of light as better than night, in that it is the aspect of the illusory world of human experience that is closer to reality, to being, than is night. Proof of that depends on connections between (1) the language Parmenides employed when speaking of light and night and (2) words he used in the Way of Truth. (For instance, he began the poem by talking of his learning experience as a passage from night to light, from ignorance to knowledge.)

AFTER PARMENIDES

Parmenides argued that certain human ways of talking and thinking are absurd, nonsense. Since science had adopted those same ways of talking and thinking, it followed that the physicists had also been talking nonsense.

It might be thought that no one paid any serious attention to what he had to say. There *were* poets and wits who laughed and made fun of his views and, in that very limited fashion, "defended" the ordinary ways of thinking. But in order to understand what next came to pass in Greek philosophy, it must be realized that within the small yet growing intellectual community, Parmenides was taken very seriously indeed. Whatever those succeeding thinkers may have thought of his conclusions, his powerful arguments had to be taken into account. Even that is too weak a way of putting it: The next stage of development of philosophy was wholly dominated by the attempt to come to grips with Parmenides.

The philosophical community made three types of response to the Parmenidean position. First, some philosophers defended the kind of view developed by Parmenides. Second, rather than causing the young scientific tradition to dry up, Parmenidean metaphysics in fact stimulated the development of some of the most important Greek cosmological schemes. Last, some came to regard the dispute about reality as essentially unsolvable and so turned their attention to other intellectual pursuits.

I shall take up those responses and the individuals who embodied them in succeeding chapters.

As Parmenides was born about 515 B.C.E., his poem must have been written soon after the first decade of the fifth century B.C.E., roughly at the time of the Persian Wars. Moreover, those who were then forced to make some response to him were fifth-century thinkers, people who were born after the turn of the century. Thus, the debate caused by Parmenides is central to the development of philosophy in the fifth century B.C.E.

BIBLIOGRAPHY

Montgomery Furth, "Elements of Eleatic Ontology," reprinted in A. P. D. Mourelatos, ed., *The Pre-Socratics* (Garden City, N.Y.: Anchor Books, 1974).
    This paper and Owen's "Eleatic Questions" (next entry) are difficult but are the essays on Parmenides I have found most insightful.
G. E. L. Owen, "Eleatic Questions," reprinted in R. E. Allen and David Furley, eds., *Studies in Presocratic Philosophy*, Vol. 2 (Atlantic Highlands, N.J.: Humanities Press, 1975).
A. P. D. Mourelatos, *The Route of Parmenides* (New Haven, Conn.: Yale University Press, 1970).
    Difficult but good on the literary aspects of Parmenides.

9

THE ELEATICS: ZENO

Parmenides was a native of the Italian *polis* of Elea. He had two disciples who acquired their own philosophical importance. Since the three shared Parmenides' philosophical outlook, they are often called the Eleatics and their philosophy Eleaticism.

Not only did those two, Zeno *(Zee'-no)* and Melissus *(Meh-liss'-us)*, accept the general correctness of the metaphysical view developed by Parmenides, they also followed the master in using patterns of deductive argument. Eleatic philosophy was as much marked by its logical rigor as by its characteristic philosophical theses. Eleatic writings bristle with argumentation. With the exception of the Prologue to Parmenides' poem, their work consists of no narrative or other such relaxed modes of writing, but is completely given over to argumentation.

While both students acquired some philosophical standing of their own, Zeno is by far the most important and is the one who must be given detailed treatment here. From Aristotle onward, Melissus has been criticized as second-rate. He had the intellectual misfortune to accept the views of a very powerful and very original mind and thus, thinking and working within the Parmenidean "paradigm" or "research tradition" (as such things have come to be called), could only contribute alterations to the overall scheme. (A major alteration concerned space. He saw that Parmenides' belief that the universe is limited, finite, must face the question "What happens at the spatial edge of the universe?" Moreover, by ceasing to think about the question of the universe's limits as a *moral* issue [whether it is good and right that the universe should exist within limits], Melissus furthered the Pre-Socratic development of a *naturalistic* account of the world in which we live.)

ZENO

Melissus was as systematic a thinker as Parmenides. The system he defended, however, was only a modified version of that produced by his master, and consequently Melissus has never achieved the status of a major thinker. Parmenides' second disciple, Zeno (a native of Elea), also aimed at supporting Parmenides' teachings, but his strategy was radically different from that of Melissus. It was partially Zeno's argumentative strategy that has earned him an important place not just in the history of Pre-Socratic philosophy but also in Western thought as a whole. Furthermore, in exercising those argumentative techniques, he created the famous Zeno's Paradoxes.

We have already met Zeno: in Plato's dialogue the *Parmenides,* Parmenides is reported to have come to Athens for a great festival about 450 B.C.E., bringing with him his pupil Zeno, who is said to have been about forty years old at the time. Plato says that as a young man Zeno had published a book that had given him a certain reputation. However, years later the book had not reached Athens, though Zeno's reputation had, so he was asked to give a public reading of the work while in Athens. Socrates attended this reading and questioned Zeno about his aims and methods.

In Plato's account—and the history of interpreting Zeno has concurred—the aim of Zeno's book was to defend Parmenides' monism. But Zeno did not go about that task in the same way that Melissus did. That is, he did not advance Parmenidean-type proofs of the proposition that there can be only one thing. Rather, he set out to attack denials of monism. Zeno's project was to show that *pluralism is absurd.* Given this reading of his purpose, Zeno is not a constructive thinker, not a system builder, such as was Parmenides (and even Melissus), but a *critic,* one whose aim is to show that a particular intellectual position is untenable.

Zeno employed a technique that has helped to make him famous. It now bears the (Latin) name *reductio ad absurdum*—sometimes shortened to *reductio.*

This form of argument is designed to show that some supposition or hypothesis or belief is impossible or absurd. Its ideal form is "Suppose H (some hypothesis about something) is true. If H were true, then Conclusion 1 and Conclusion 2 would also be true. But C1 and C2 *can't both* be true. Therefore, H cannot be true." It is thus argued that a hypothesis leads to two different and contradictory consequences and is thus false because it reduces to an impossible state of affairs.

Zeno probably did not invent that argumentative technique. No doubt people had long since used the more general form of that argument (what logicians call *modus tollens*); for example, "Look: if the Greeks *had* already landed, they would have pillaged the town; but as you can see, everything is perfectly normal here; so they can't have arrived yet." Moreover, there is some reason to believe that Greek mathematicians had already begun to argue by *reductio,* that is, to use that special form of *modus tollens* that is the *reductio* to show that a given mathematical hypothesis has contradictory consequences and thus cannot be true. Like Parmenides, Zeno is presumed to have had some connection with the Pythagorean mathematicians in the vicinity of Elea. So probably Zeno did not create the method. His contribution seems to have been the realization that the *reductio* could be systematically employed as an intellectual weapon.

The aim, then, was to argue against pluralism by using *reductio* arguments. Pluralism is the view that the world is composed of many different things. Thus, Zeno would argue, "Let us grant that you are correct, that there are many things. Then thus and thus consequences follow. But those consequences are impossible (contradictory). So there cannot be many things: pluralism is impossible, absurd." Probably the book was composed of nothing but a string of *reductio* arguments against pluralism. (Plato says Socrates had to ask for clarification of what the point of the book was despite just having heard it read.) There is testimony that it consisted of *forty* such arguments against pluralism. Only two have been transmitted to us in Zeno's own words, and we possess hints about two others.

Zeno's reputation does not rest on the idea that he produced philosophically interesting objections to pluralism. To think that forty or so important and distinct objections can be made to the idea that the world contains many things strains belief. It is much more likely that Zeno was employing a shotgun technique and firing without much regard for the detailed acceptability of the arguments he produced, intending rather to overwhelm his opponents, unaccustomed as they probably were to the rigors of deductive reasoning, by sheer weight of numbers. That certainly accords with Plato's understanding of Zeno as a logic-chopper, a person who treats argument as a contest and not as a (or the) path to truth.

Yet more recent scholarship has tended to suggest that at least one of the existent objections to plurality—in which Zeno argues that if there are many things, then everything has no size at all and yet everything would be infinitely large—is more important than historically assumed, because it underlies Zeno's objections to motion. However, since the arguments about motion are the basis of his reputation, I must devote the limited space available to them.

The Paradoxes of Motion

Aristotle has preserved for us, though not in the original words, Zeno's four arguments against motion. These famous *paradoxes* do not seem to have been part of the original book, if it was directed against plurality only; yet despite the mention in later antiquity of other titles by Zeno, the evidence is not strong that there were books corresponding to the titles. Hence we know nothing about where and when Zeno produced the arguments.

These paradoxes were famous in the ancient world, playing a role in the debate initiated by Parmenides concerning space and motion. Nonetheless, both then and throughout many centuries following, they were held to be mere sophisms, verbal tricks and quibbles, not to be taken seriously. Only in the last hundred years has that estimate changed. The paradoxes have come to be regarded in this century as containing exquisitely subtle problems of deep concern not only to philosophy but also to modern mathematics and physics:

> The paradoxes of Zeno of Elea are objects of beauty and charm, and sources of intense intellectual excitement. Using everyday occurrences, such as a footrace or the flight of an arrow, Zeno shows that simple considerations lead to profound difficulties. In his attempt to demonstrate the impossibility of plurality, motion, and change, he points to problems lying at the very heart of our concepts of space, time, motion, continuity, and infinity. Since these concepts play fundamental roles in philosophy, mathematics, and physics, the implications of the paradoxes are far-reaching indeed. It is perhaps amusing to be confronted by a simple argument which purports to demonstrate the unreality of something as obviously real as motion; it is deeply intriguing to find that the resolution of the paradox requires the subtlety of modern physics, mathematics and philosophy. It is difficult to think of any other problem in science or philosophy which can be stated so simply and whose resolution carries one so far or so deep. (Salmon, 1970, p. 5)

INTERPRETIVE ISSUES

Several important problems about understanding Zeno's arguments need mention before we attend to the arguments themselves.

1. A major dispute has concerned whether Zeno had the Pythagoreans in mind as the major opponents when he created these arguments (and those against pluralism, too). I suspect that he did not, but nothing in the following discussion depends on either answer to the question.

2. It has also been asserted that the four paradoxes were not independent of each other, but that Zeno carefully constructed them to eliminate the only four reasonable defenses of motion. In any *full* account of them, questions about the interrelationships of the paradoxes must be addressed. In the account following, I will pass over those matters.

3. Again, critical discussions of the paradoxes may well require becoming deeply involved in their relation to contemporary mathematical physics. However, time and space here are insufficient to develop those connections.

4. Lastly, the strong recent appreciation of the paradoxes has not arisen because philosophers believe that they really do show that motion is impossible. Rather, some philosophers think that in trying to resolve the paradoxes successfully—that is, in showing how they do *not* establish that motion cannot occur—we are led to raise deep questions about space, continuity, infinity, and so on. The question is not so much what Zeno had in mind when he proposed the paradoxes, but what we must say and think in order to escape them.

Parmenides asserted that change is impossible. Thus motion, change of place, is not possible. Nothing can move. His opponents, whether philosophers or not, would say that is absurd—obviously things *do* move. Zeno intends to show that *the idea* that things move is *itself* an absurd belief.

He has been held to have conducted all his argumentation in terms of *reductios*. Thus the paradoxes are presumed to have the general form "Suppose motion is possible; then it follows that C and not-C; but that is absurd, impossible; hence, there cannot be motion."

However, it is much more difficult to set what we possess of the arguments against motion in that form than to do so for the arguments against plurality. That difficulty may be due to the fact that we have only Aristotle's paraphrases of them, not the originals. Still, most interpreters do not try to cast them into the paradigm form of a *reductio*, and I shall not be overly conscientious about doing so here. Nonetheless, they are obviously attempts to show that belief in the possibility of motion is absurd.

The Achilles

I shall take as my chief specimen of the paradoxes what has been called since antiquity the Achilles. Aristotle states it thus: "This is the argument that the slowest runner cannot be caught by the fastest. For the pursuer must first reach where the pursued started, so that the slower will always be some distance ahead."

That is clearly only the barest bones of the argument. The first step must be to put some flesh on, to make explicit some of the obvious assumptions of that version. Since antiquity, the argument has not simply been fleshed out but has been dramatized.

Suppose a race is to be held between someone slower and someone faster. Since Achilles was the fastest of the Greeks, let one of the runners be him— and let the other be that slowest of the slow, a tortoise. As we already know that Achilles is much faster than the tortoise, to make the race interesting let us give the tortoise a head start of some length. At the starting gun, they both begin to run. Let us assume for simplicity of presentation that both are seriously interested in the race and continue to run throughout at top speed.

Our ordinary belief is that, all things being equal (Achilles does not pull a hamstring, the head start is not too great for the race distance, and so on), Achilles will overtake and pass the tortoise. But Zeno argues that, on the contrary, even if none of those eventualities should come to pass, even if the race proceeds normally, Achilles cannot catch up to the tortoise, much less pass it.

The interest, of course, lies in how he argues that it is impossible for the faster to overtake the slower. To see that, let us continue spelling out the quote from Aristotle.

Given that the slower, the tortoise, has a head start and that both run the race seriously, then at some time Achilles will reach that spot from which the tortoise began the race. But at the time when Achilles gets to that spot, where will the tortoise be? On the assumptions made about the race, it will have covered some distance while Achilles has been running and so will not be at its starting place. That is, the tortoise will still be ahead. The race thus continues. To catch the tortoise, Achilles must then reach the place at which the tortoise was when he reached its starting place. But during the interval when he was covering *that* distance, the tortoise once again has covered *some* distance. So while he is closer, the tortoise is still ahead. Achilles continues to run, but each time, on reaching the place where the tortoise was, finds that it has again moved some distance ahead. Consequently, he can never catch up, he is always some, increasingly small but never vanishing, distance behind. Hence, the faster cannot catch the slower. (The reader should attempt to draw a picture of this argument—of the race—if there is any doubt about what Zeno is claiming.)

If one wanted to cast the whole into the form of a *reductio,* it would go something like this: "Suppose that motion is possible, that things can move. If it makes sense to speak of things moving, it makes sense to say that things can move at different speeds. Consequently, if one object's speed is greater than another, it will eventually overtake and pass the other. But equally, if we analyze (as we just did) what is involved in one object overtaking another, we can see that it is impossible for that to happen. Hence, the idea that motion can occur, since it allows the intelligibility of talk of different speeds, implies both that faster things can and cannot overtake things moving at a slower speed. That is a contradiction. Hence, since the concept of motion leads to contradictory consequences, there cannot be such a thing as motion."

A philosopher's impulse is to pause here in order to take the argument apart, to see how such a paradoxical conclusion as that of the Achilles is generated. Sadly, such detailed analysis and evaluation of arguments is not the aim of this book. Nonetheless, something further needs to be said here to show how science and mathematics get hooked into resolving the paradoxes. Nothing yet said shows anything about any potential role for them. The following constitutes a beginning sketch of how these further studies are relevant to discussions of Zeno's argument.

Zeno's account of the race contains an assumption as to how Achilles proceeds. He is described as running from Point 1 (his starting place) to Point 2 (the tortoise's starting place) and from there to Point 3 (where the tortoise was when he got to Point 2) and so on. The argument, that is, takes it that motion is to be understood as proceeding through a sequence of points. The problem for Achilles is that since the tortoise is always moving, there is *always* one more point for him to pass through before he overtakes the other runner, namely, the point at which the tortoise is when Achilles begins toward it. To say that there is *always* one more point that Achilles must reach for him to catch the tortoise is to say that he must pass through an infinite sequence of points to catch up. It is the same as the attempt to count through the sequence of positive integers (1, 2, 3, . . .): no matter which number you have reached, there is always one more number to go. Consequently, you cannot reach the end of the number series by counting. So too Achilles cannot reach the tortoise by running, since one more point must always be attained.

Clearly, in such an analysis of the argument, mathematical issues arise: questions about points and infinite sequences and convergent series are relevant. But further, questions about how space is to be understood, about whether it is to be analyzed as a collection of points or as continuous, also arise. And such problems about the proper mathematical analysis of space are questions of physics.

The Dichotomy

I shall content myself with giving an even more abbreviated account of Zeno's three further objections to motion than that given for the Achilles.

Aristotle cites as the first of Zeno's arguments one usually called the Dichotomy. Commentators usually say that it came in two different forms, although the two probably amount to the same thing.

Version 1 argues that, for instance, Achilles cannot even reach the place from which the tortoise began (much less catch it). To get there, he must cover half the distance first, and then cover half the remaining distance, and then half of that, and so on and on. In short, there will always be some distance he has not yet traversed between his present position and the tortoise's starting point and hence he cannot reach that point.

The other version argues that Achilles, for instance, could not even begin the race. For to get halfway to the tortoise's starting place, he must first cover half that distance, and to cross that first half, he must first cover half of it, and to do that half, he must first . . . That is, one must cross an infinite number of distances to get anywhere. But since taking one step is getting somewhere, Achilles cannot take even one step. Motion is impossible.

In both cases Zeno is arguing that while the concept of motion implies that a moving body will proceed from Point A to Point B, moving from Point A to Point B also requires that an infinite number of prior steps be taken. As an infinite sequence cannot be completed, it is impossible for a thing to move. Thus, the concept of motion is contradictory.

The Arrow

The following is a somewhat free rendition of Zeno's third paradox, called the Arrow. Consider an arrow in flight. As is true of all objects, at every moment it must be in the place where it is and in no other. Yet the moving arrow, as with all objects in motion, in order to be moving must be going from place to place. So it must at every moment be *in* a place and yet must be *going from* place to place. That state of affairs is contradictory, and a concept that entails a contradiction cannot be intelligible.

The Stadium

Zeno's final paradox of motion (usually called the Stadium but sometimes called the Moving Rows) can be stated in a variety of equivalent ways, all of which cry out for a diagram. Let me also dramatize the argument with a story impossible for Zeno. Suppose there are three parallel sets of train tracks—on Track A, the freight cars are stationary; on Track B, they are moving in the direction indicated; and on Track C, the train is moving in the opposite direction. Moreover, assume, first, that Trains B and C are traveling at the same speed and, second, that all the cars of all the trains are of equal size—say 10 feet long. Let us suppose that at the start of the story the trains are arranged as follows:

		A1	A2		

			B1	B2	

	C2	C1			

Now let us say that one minute later Trains B and C have moved to the following positions:

		A1	A2		

		B1	B2		

		C2	C1		

Zeno asked, essentially, what distance Train B has moved in that minute. Car B1 has moved to be precisely opposite Car A1, and as each car is 10 feet long, B has covered 10 feet in that minute. But notice that B1 has also completely passed Car C1 and come precisely opposite Car C2. As each of those is just 10 feet long, B has covered 20 feet in that same minute.

So B has moved 10 feet and also 20 feet during the same minute. In general, a moving thing will cover both n and $2n$ units of distance at one and the same time. Yet that is contradictory. Hence, the concept of motion produces yet another contradiction and so is useless.

ZENO AND PHILOSOPHY

Zeno has become important for the paradoxes. Yet of even broader significance has been his style of philosophizing. I said earlier that Zeno was not the type of philosopher who constructed systems of the world, but was instead a *critic*. Moreover, clearly Zeno did not merely attack the views of others—he also relished the activity of refuting others.

Both the procedure and the enjoyment of it became central to Greek philosophy in the fifth century. The Sophists (to be discussed later) were strongly influenced by the Zeno who saw philosophy as a verbal game, as a contest of argumentation. And Socrates, who shared so much with the Sophists, took over wholesale Zeno's *reductio* technique and made it the center of his life and philosophical activity—although his motives for engaging in projects of refutation were not precisely those of Zeno and the Sophists.

Through Socrates, Zeno's intellectual style has strongly shaped the whole of Western philosophy. In one picture, the philosopher is the wise person, the lover of wisdom who strives to see the most general truths about the world. But the model derived from Zeno is quite different: here the philosopher is destructive, out to demolish the views of others (and may well enjoy doing so). It is impossible to understand the practice of philosophy unless one sees that both models, the philosopher as contemplator of truth and as a participant in an intellectual war, have been present from Zeno onward.

BIBLIOGRAPHY

Wesley C. Salmon, ed., *Zeno's Paradoxes* (Indianapolis, Ind.: Bobbs-Merrill, 1970).
An anthology of important essays on Zeno's paradoxes with an extensive bibliography.
J. A. Faris, *The Paradoxes of Zeno* (Brookfield, Vt.: Ashgate Publishing, 1996).
A good recent discussion of the paradoxes.

10

REDOING SCIENCE

Philosophy began with cosmological and cosmogonical problems. But after slightly more than a hundred years of vigorous intellectual expansion, a philosopher was produced whose powerfully reasoned views, if true, made cosmology and cosmogony impossible. If only one thing can exist, a thing that has no properties, cannot change, has no past and no future—then there is nothing on which science can be practiced.

Such outlandish views, of course, were not attractive to many. The young cosmological tradition did not just dry up and go away. Rather, a major resurgence of science followed Parmenides. In fact, considerable time had elapsed since a major scientific system had been produced (Anaximenes had been the last). Nevertheless, after Parmenides, and presumably because of him, several of the most striking ancient Greek cosmologies were proposed.

REPLYING TO PARMENIDES

The general problem facing this revival of science was what to do about Parmenides, about the Eleatic contentions. On the one hand, most of those conclusions were not believable. On the other, this next generation of thinkers could not imagine dealing with the Eleatics as Aristotle and modern scientists would do: namely, by leaving the task of answering such wild views to the philosophers. (Aristotle, *Physics* 184b25–185a17: "Asking whether Being is one and motionless is not part of the science of nature. . . . We physicists must assume that natural objects, all or some, are in motion. . . . Moreover, scientists are not required to resolve every kind of issue that can arise, only those which seem to follow from the principles of their own science: we are not in the business of refuting other views.") Not having a distinction between philosophy and physics, the post-Parmenidean cosmologists felt responsible for making a reply.

Unhappily for them, the philosophical tools to refute Parmenides' position had not yet been created. So they could not believe the Parmenidean conclusions, and could not ignore them, but had not the means for demonstrating the errors of reasoning that the Eleatic arguments must contain.

What options were thus available? Cosmologists might have followed the lead of Parmenides himself and claimed that while nothing further could be said about *reality*, a scientific account could be produced of the world *as it mistakenly appears to human senses*. That way out was tempting but not genuinely palatable to those with scientific ambitions.

With no good options available, they did the next best thing: they did the best they could. They refused to take seriously some of Parmenides' conclusions, especially his monism. They accepted some of his theses and modified the basic principles of the inherited scientific systems, in an attempt to meet the requirements imposed by those theses. In short, they staggered along.

These compromise cosmologies are strange mixtures of failure and genius. None of them can solve the problems their creators took on, for what must be responded to were Parmenides' arguments, and the philosophical tools to do that had not yet been created. Yet in their attempt to do science with Parmenides in mind, the new scientists were genuinely and deeply creative, arriving at fruitful ideas even if these could not succeed as refutations of Parmenides.

There are three major attempts to recreate the Ionian practice of inquiry into the cosmos in light of Parmenides' criticism of the assumptions it shared with the ordinary run of humankind. Two were produced by individual men, Anaxagoras *(Ann-axe-agg'-oras)* and Empedocles *(Em-ped'-o-klees)*, and the third, called Atomism, was a joint product of Leucippus *(Lew-kipp' -us)* and Democritus *(Deh-mock'-reet-us)*. Also note that some of the major embellishments of Pythagorean cosmology were added at this time, perhaps in response to Parmenides. In that development of Pythagoreanism the key figure is Philolaus. Since I have woven the discussion of those matters into my discussion of Pythagoras, I shall concentrate here on the reconstruction of Ionian scientific thought.

PLURALISM

These various attempts to modify the old Ionian science in order to evade Parmenides shared two important features.

One common characteristic of the new systems is their pluralism with respect to the ultimate material constituents of the universe. The earliest Ionian cosmologies had tried to generate the universe and all its objects out of *one* fundamental kind of stuff, although they differed about what that initial stuff was.

After Parmenides, that older monism was finished. The new pluralists held that the world is formed of *several* equally ultimate stuffs. (Parmenides himself, in his cosmology of appearances, may have suggested that.) That pluralism is characteristic of these post-Parmenidean systems.

These thinkers believed that they could avoid Parmenidean snares by *postulating* an original, uncreated plurality of different stuffs. The idea that the cosmic game had started with several pieces on the board cleverly meets (part of) the Eleatic point that coming to be is impossible. Nonetheless, it completely fails to respond to the arguments that there can be only one thing. The pluralism is assumed, not argued for.

CAUSATION

In describing a cosmos in which change was a prominent feature, the older cosmologists had given no explanation of *why* the stuff of the world changes. They seem to have assumed that no explanation is called for, that it is in the nature of the primary stuff to transform itself.

Post-Parmenidean science made a quite different assumption. The stuffs composing the world were now taken to be incapable of self-initiated change. Matter is no longer thought to be alive, that is, capable of moving itself. Therefore, the cosmologist must face the question of why change comes about. Although the Atomists were not in full agreement, it was then generally assumed that the causes of alterations in nature are to be sought in some source external to the material constituents.

The new attention to problems of causation was no doubt the result of a belief that such a concern is necessary to escape Eleatic objections to change. However, the distinction between stuff and cause could not succeed in getting away from arguments against change: Parmenides' denial of the possibility of change could not be replied to by talking about causation.

FAILURE AND PROGRESS

Thus, the two chief maneuvers executed to escape Parmenides did not work. Nonetheless, such moves were progressive. It no longer was simply assumed that the best account of the world could make do with *one* ultimate stuff. Scientists could begin to wonder how many fundamental types of matter are necessary to account for the variety of things we find in nature. And it was a fruitful move, a genuine intellectual advance, to recognize a distinction between causes and material constituents. On those grounds alone, the post-Parmenidean cosmological renewal was a major event in the history of Greek philosophy. Failure and progress often go together.

EMPEDOCLES

Although Anaxagoras was slightly older than Empedocles (who lived, on the best estimation, from 492 to 432 B.C.E.), it is most helpful to start an account of the renewal of the cosmological tradition with the younger of the two men.

Empedocles was a Western Greek, a citizen of an important Sicilian *polis*, Acragas. He was reputed to be a many-sided genius with a striking personality. Guthrie calls him "one of the most complex and colorful figures of antiquity," indeed "one of the most remarkable individuals of any period" (Vol. 2, p. 123). Empedocles was not given to humility:

> Friends, who live in great Acragas which looks down from the heights on the yellow river, concerned as you are with fine deeds, providers of refuge for strangers, unacquainted with want, Greetings! I go among you no longer a mortal, but an immortal god, honored as is proper, crowned with ribbons and flowers. When I enter prosperous cities, I am revered by men and women. People follow me by the thousands, some asking advice on acquiring riches, some seeking prophecies, others, victims of suffering, begging for the word which will heal their various afflictions. (Fragment 112)

He promised to transfer his own powers to his friend to whom he addressed his poem on the system of nature:

> You shall learn all drugs to ward off illness and aging—for you alone will I do all this. You shall learn how to stop the unstoppable winds which blast the earth and destroy the crops; and, if you wish, you shall be able to have them blow again. You shall learn to stop the dark rains when they have gone on too long for the needs of mankind and to make them pour from the sky to nourish the trees after the summer drought. You shall have the power to bring the dead back to life. (Fragment 111)

Against Empedocles' own arrogance must be set his politics, for he was deeply involved in the political transformation of Acragas from a tyranny to a democracy. Later he was forced into exile by his political enemies.

In the ancient world, he was highly regarded as an orator; Aristotle called him the inventor of the art of rhetoric.

His writings clearly show that the theory and practice of medicine was a central concern of his, although, as the fragments quoted earlier show, both drugs and faith-healing were in his medical arsenal. In fact, he made important contributions to Greek medical theory and was the source of an important Sicilian medical tradition.

He was the last of the Greek philosophers who cast their work into epic form. Unlike Parmenides, Empedocles was a very good poet, good enough for Aristotle to accuse him of writing better than he thought. Nonetheless, his epic about the fall and rise of the universe and its companion about the fall and rise of the *psyché* are both poetically excellent and intellectually powerful. Of those two poems, reputed to have originally consisted of about 5,000 lines, nearly 450 lines have survived, which means that while we possess more of his texts than of any other Pre-Socratic philosopher, we have less than 10 percent of what he wrote.

Empedocles the Cosmologist

Political activist, medical thinker and wonder-worker, rhetorician, poet, seeker after and theoretician of salvation—Empedocles was all these and more. He was also one of the major philosopher-cosmologists of the Greek world. Although he was a Western Greek, deeply influenced by Pythagoreanism, especially in its religious aspect, the content of his philosophical work was nonetheless an adaptation of the Ionian cosmological tradition. That is, mathematics is not central in his account of the history and functioning of the world (though it does have an important role). Instead, Ionian matter theory was the background to his system.

Empedocles set out to adapt that type of theory to the changed circumstances produced by Parmenides. Empedocles, in his cosmological epic *On Nature*, intentionally employs Parmenidean language to indicate where he thinks one must agree with Parmenides. His problem is, then, how to accept *that* much of the Eleatic position and yet provide an Ionian account of the nature and development of the world.

The Parmenidean Requirements

Empedocles accepts the following Eleatic theses: "[Mortals are] fools. They do not think deeply, for they fancy that what at one time was not can come to be and that things can perish and be completely destroyed. It is impossible that anything should come to be from what is not and it is impossible, unthinkable, that what is should be annihilated" (Fragments 11 and 12).

Those theses are the starting place for Empedocles' cosmic system. He considers that Parmenides has established that nothing new can come into being and that what is cannot pass away. He will attempt to produce a cosmological theory that satisfies those conditions.

The Solution: The Four Roots

In seeing how Empedocles constructed a system of the world that meets those requirements, let us for now restrict the discussion to the basic stuffs of the world.

The Ionians had held that there was but one fundamental kind of stuff, which is transformed into the other cosmic stuffs (as well as becoming everything else, in the long run). For example, in a system in which water is the original stuff, the other stuffs—earth, air, and fire—came into being as merely altered states of the original. If air was held to be the *arché,* then earth, water, and fire were derived from air.

Empedocles, agreeing with Parmenides that it is impossible to get something from something else, rejected such transformations. But he also made the Ionian assumption that the world is obviously composed of earth, air, fire, and water. Those two assumptions can be made compatible by holding that they must all be equally primitive cosmic constituents. Thus, for Empedocles, the universe consists of four equally basic types of stuff. (It is possible to say that Empedocles, borrowing from Parmenides' Way of

Appearance, created the idea of an *element,* a basic form of matter that cannot be transformed into some other stuff.)

These stuffs—or *roots,* as Empedocles called them—are held to be uncreated, indestructible, and unchangeable. In these respects, they are just like the Parmenidean One—except that there are four. They differ also from that One in another way: they are not featureless, for they have qualities, properties. In fact, they are qualitatively different (water *is* watery and *is not* earthy or fiery).

Empedocles accepts two more contentions of Parmenides. "Nor is any part of the whole empty" (Empedocles, Fragment 13). That is, space is full of "what is"; there is no void. And Fragments 28 and 29 echo Parmenides in declaring "what is" to be a well-rounded sphere.

Hence the world, in this first description, consists of the four roots, which are stuffs with different properties, organized spherically and completely filling that spherical space.

Introducing Change

A world as simple as that is as impervious to scientific inquiry as the billiard ball universe of Parmenides. If there is to be science, there must be more to the world. To put the issue differently, what about the diversity of objects and changes we find in the world? The Ionian cosmologists attempted to make sense of these objects and alterations. What is their status in Empedocles' scheme?

Empedocles agreed that "what is" cannot come into being nor can it pass away. Hence he was committed to saying that the comings and goings we find in our sensory experience cannot really be how things are. But is what we experience illusion, appearance, as Parmenides held? Empedocles could not accept that account of it, either.

On the one hand, he wanted to insist that the only things that really *are,* are the elements (as Fragments 17 and 21 say). Nonetheless, he wanted to talk about (and, if there is to be science, must talk about) *other substances* such as wine and gold and wood, and also about *particular objects* such as a bottle or a ring or a tree. As a scientist, he found it unthinkable that those items are mere illusion.

He needed and found what he thought to be an acceptable solution to those seemingly incompatible demands: "I will tell you another thing: there is no birth for mortal things, nor any hateful death, but only mixing and separating of what has been mixed—'birth' is the name given to that by men" (Fragment 8). That is, only the elements are real. But they do mix together, the result being such mixtures as gold and such objects as horses. According to Empedocles, that is not really the creation of anything new—people only call it that. Nor is the destruction of a horse nor the burning of wood the passing away of anything, although human beings do talk that way. What is thought to be destruction is only the separation of a mixture back into the elements.

That solution looks clever, but it won't work against the Eleatics. If you take flour, sugar, milk, chocolate, and so on, and mix them up to make a cake, when the project is finished something exists that did not exist before: a cake. And when the cake is consumed or fragmented or dissolved, there is no longer what there was, namely the cake. Commingling and separating are not processes different from bringing into being and destroying as Empedocles tried to make out. They are ways of creating and destroying things.

In fact, when Empedocles gets down to work, that attempted distinction between creation-destruction and mixing-separating plays no role in his cosmology. He continually speaks of *mortal* things and also thinks of them as being generated and destroyed. As Fragment 17 says in part, "There is a twofold generation of mortal things and a twofold passing away," and Fragment 71 says, in the same spirit, "How by the mixing of water, earth, air and sun there came to be the shapes and colors of those mortal things which now exist. . . ." (Notice that he there allows not only *things* to come to be but also *properties,* qualities: there *are* "changes of bright color," and so on.) He knows that he talks that way and attempts to justify it by saying "I too use those terms as is customary" (Fragment 9); he is merely following the deceitful customs of mortal language. As we have seen, it is not merely a false human practice to speak of creation where mixture is involved, because mixing *is* a way of bringing into being.

Instead of concentrating on Empedoclean shortcomings with respect to Parmenides' position, it is now time to set those aside and concentrate on Empedocles' creativity in developing a cosmological system.

Empedoclean Chemistry
Obviously, the foregoing shows Empedocles thought that the creation of mortal items of the world from the uncreated roots is accomplished by mixing those elements together, while their destruction is the reverse process: separating what was mixed together back into its elemental constituents.

Using composition and decomposition to explain coming to be and passing away probably goes back to Anaximander and was certainly employed by Parmenides in his cosmology of appearances. Empedocles, however, made the use of those notions much more specific. He attempted to account for the differences between nonultimate stuffs by specifying differing *proportions* of the elemental stuffs that went into them as their ingredients. And he even gave a few examples. Thus in Fragment 96 he specifies that bone is comprised of four parts fire, two parts water, and two parts earth.

Although Empedocles' Pythagorean heritage supplied him with the idea of explaining differences in terms of proportions, the use he made of it in connection with Ionian matter theory was highly original. He thereby created what has been called "the chemical conception of matter." Although his elements differed from those of today's chemistry, he was the ancestor of such modern chemical conceptions as that the nature of, say, sulfuric acid is expressible as a formula, H_2SO_4.

Later chemical theory held that ultimate units of the elements are combined in producing other stuffs. Modern chemistry says that 2 *atoms* of hydrogen unite with 1 *atom* of oxygen to form water. When Empedocles said that bone consists of four parts fire, two parts water, and so on, did he have in mind that those parts are some minimal amount or smallest piece of the element in question? The evidence does not allow a definitive answer. He certainly must have thought that the four elements come in the form of smallish pieces, but he probably did not have the idea that there is some minimal unit of the stuff.

The Forces

Mixing creates and separating destroys mortal stuffs. What does the mixing and separating? Empedocles was the first of the cosmologists to invoke the idea of an *agency* other than the stuff itself in the explanation of natural changes. Anaximenes, for example, explained alterations in nature as the outcome of the expansion and contraction of the basic stuff, air. Why did air behave like that? The question was not asked and hence not answered. Empedocles, no doubt believing that he could thereby sidestep Parmenides' argument against change, held that the stuffs do not just mix and separate themselves. Rather, there are two further cosmic constituents whose function is to shuffle the elements about so as to form mixtures and to break them down once again.

For Empedocles, *six* ultimate items furnish the world: the four roots or stuffs and two equally uncreated and indestructible forces or powers.

Empedocles calls these two forces *love* and *strife*. They have very specific functions. It is wrong to think of one as the force of attraction and the other as one that repels. Each is a principle of attraction: love attracts unlike elements into combinations—that is, love is what mixes all four elements together—while strife is the principle by which like is attracted to like and thus is what pulls units of water, say, away from units of earth and into combination with other units of water.

Love and strife must not be thought of as sheerly *mechanical* forces such as gravity or magnetic fields, which act on purely inert matter. Empedocles not only called the four roots fire, air, and so on, but he also gave them mythological names. Thus he thought of them as divine, hence living, entities. He also called love "Aphrodite" and clearly thought of the principle that creates things by attracting different elements to merge as exactly the same principle that produces sexual desire in a human being. Nonetheless, while the components of the cosmos were not totally naturalized, demythologized, by Empedocles, it is not a long step from his characterization of them to a fully naturalistic view.

Not only did he not have a clear conception of the forces as mechanical, but he was also not fully able to make a clear distinction between a stuff and a force. Some of his characterizations of love and strife sound as though he regarded them as very special kinds of stuff.

The Cosmic Cycle

There is decent evidence that Anaximander believed in a great cycle wherein every so often the stuffs that make up the cosmos are drawn back into the *apeiron,* only to be separated off again to begin the formation of yet another organized world. Some evidence shows that Heraclitus had a similar idea, that there is a cycle in which the world as we know it is destroyed by fire only to be reconstituted later. The orthodox interpretation of Empedocles' system has been that this idea of a cycle was the central feature of his cosmogony. That account has been vigorously disputed in recent years, but, I think, not shown to be wrong. Hence I shall adopt that interpretation here.

Empedocles posited two polar stages in the alteration of the world. In one, love has become fully dominant so that the four elements are totally scrambled together (recall that the shape here is that of a sphere). At the other end, strife is wholly in control so that the sphere is organized into four perfectly concentric areas, each area consisting of only one element.

The world, then, cycles back and forth between those two poles, an organized cosmos being created in each transition period. In consequence, a cosmos, a mortal world of mortal things, results only when *both* the opposing forces, love and strife, are active, a picture very reminiscent of Heraclitus' view of the creative function of opposition. Without the activity of both forces, there is either perfect chaos or perfect order—neither condition being that of a cosmos.

Within this framework, Empedocles attempted to carry out Anaximander's project of a comprehensive account of our world. The limits of this book forbid any attempt to give a full account of his views on the various scientific issues he considered, so what follows is a quick survey.

Empedocles held that we live in the transition phase between love and strife. In fact, things are fairly far along toward the dominance of strife. Consequently, he told a story of the development of the cosmos from the state of love's dominance to the present.

Embedded in that account are astronomical and geological theories, that is, discussions of the nature and behavior of heavenly bodies and of prominent features of the earth. He provides a more complex account than had Anaximander of the evolution of living creatures (even suggesting that natural selection, though not by that name, is responsible for eliminating plants and animals other than those which presently exist). His medical and biological interests are shown in botanical, embryological, and physiological inquiries. There are psychological investigations: of the nature of thought and of the functioning of the senses. In virtually every case, his theories were important jumping-off places for later investigations of those topics.

Empedocles and Salvation

So far I have discussed Empedocles' cosmological and scientific views as they are found in the fragments of his poem *On Nature.* He was also the author of a second long poem, *Purifications,* which was not a work of science but a religious poem with an Orphic-Pythagorean outlook. The two works show connections, chiefly an intended parallel between the cosmic cycle in nature and a cycle in the spiritual life of human beings.

Once there was an age of love (when the cosmic force love was more dominant than at present). That state of innocence was broken by an original sin: the eating of flesh, which in Pythagorean fashion is considered as the eating of one's kin. In consequence, we are fallen, the penalty being a sequence of reincarnations in a variety of living, mortal forms. The only way to break free from that cycle is through various forms of purification, the most necessary of which is to abstain from eating meat.

Those religious beliefs required that we be identified with a *daimon,* a divine spirit he considers immortal. The major long-standing scholarly dispute about Empedocles concerns how he could reconcile his physical theory with his religious outlook. His account of nature *seems* to leave no room for immortal beings other than the four roots. His religious theory *seems* to require something else, a *daimon,* which is uncreated and indestructible. Many solutions have been proposed to this problem. The current consensus is that some solution must make Empedocles' views consistent. As yet, no widespread agreement exists as to precisely what that solution is.

ANAXAGORAS

It is much more difficult to produce an adequate account of Anaxagoras' cosmic system than it is for that of Empedocles. The chief difficulty in discussing Anaxagoras is not that we do not have enough information: a decent amount of his own words have survived, and the ancient testimony is extensive. Rather, the major problem is that his theory of matter is much more complex than those of his predecessors. Its complexity and subtlety fascinated even ancient commentators, and the problem has been to provide a reconstruction of his system that successfully integrates all the doctrines he seems to have held.

The fascination of piecing a sophisticated web of theses together, as well as trying to understand his arguments (Empedocles was not much of an arguer), has led scholars, ancient and modern, to spend a good deal of time working with Anaxagoras. For the beginning student, however, more can be learned of post-Parmenidean science by a good look at Empedocles. Hence, I will have less to say of Anaxagoras than the value of his views would dictate.

Back to Ionia and on to Athens

With Anaxagoras we return to the start of the story: Ionia. He came from Clazomenae *(Claz'-o-men-ee),* a *polis* just up the coast from Miletus and the other cities from which the other early philosophers came. Born about 500 B.C.E., he went to Athens when he was about twenty, shortly after the Persians were so decisively defeated in 480. The story of the growth of philosophy has so far oscillated between a narrow circle of cities in Ionia and another small group in Italy; with Anaxagoras, the focus of interest switches to Athens, for the most part to remain there.

Anaxagoras became connected with the major Athenian political figure of the great decades of the midcentury, Pericles. About 450 B.C.E., Anaxagoras was brought to trial on a charge of impiety—he had denied the divinity of the sun, declaring that it was nothing but a hot rock—but, though true, the charge was also politically motivated by Pericles' opponents. The outcome was that Anaxagoras either was exiled or fled, living until 428 across the Aegean.

He wrote a book on nature, presumably a little book since it sold for a small sum in the Athenian marketplace. The work was not poetry—it was a standard Ionian prose treatise without frills.

Anaxagoras started where Empedocles did, by accepting *some* of Parmenides' theses. He put aside Eleatic arguments for monism, because they make a system of nature fully impossible. He agreed, however, that there can be no real coming into being and passing away (and he may also have agreed that there can be no empty space). In nearly the same words as Empedocles, he holds that what people call "creation" and "extinction" are nothing but mixture and separation. His aim was to try to construct a system of nature without resorting to (real) change, by dealing only in mixture and separation of elements. (Note that from Empedocles on, we are dealing with elements somewhat as modern chemistry understands them.)

Criticism of Empedoclean-Style Solutions

It is possible, though far from certain, that Anaxagoras wrote in response to Empedocles. And in fact the best way of understanding his views is by regarding them as resulting from a critique of the Empedoclean solution to their joint problems.

Empedocles had held that mixture and separation merely rearranged the elements and did not create and destroy things. Anaxagoras was willing to accept that principle. But he objected to how Empedocles employed it. Despite Empedocles' theoretical disclaimers, Empedocles did mean that when (for example) earth, water, and fire were mixed in precise proportions, bone *came to be;* and when bone was dissolved back into its original constituents, bone had been *destroyed.* The claim that by compounding and separating one did not *really* produce or destroy stuff thus evaded the issue, because quite clearly the chemical ratios specify what this and that type of nonoriginal matter *is.*

Anaxagoras' Solution

Anaxagoras' conclusion from his analysis of the Empedoclean position was that *any* kind of stuff that is to be found in the world must, then, be a primitive, original constituent of the universe. If one seriously denies that there is any "coming to be," then everything must have been there to start with.

How many elemental types of matter are there for Anaxagoras? Not only earth, air, fire, and water, but *equally* bone, wood, copper, milk, the hot, and so on and on. He makes no attempt to provide a list. However, he uses a criterion for what counts as an element. Something is *elemental* if (and only if) the result of dividing a hunk of it into two is two hunks of the same stuff as the original. For example, a piece of gold split in two produces two pieces of gold, so gold qualifies. Chopping a pig in two does not result in two pigs, so pigs do not count as basic pieces of furniture of the universe.

For Anaxagoras, therefore, there are an *indefinitely large* number of ultimate kinds of matter, as a large number of stuffs satisfy that criterion. And *each* of these many types of matter is like the Eleatic One: uncreated, indestructible, and unchangeable.

Anaxagoras' solution, better than did Empedocles' solution, meets the requirement that a cosmic system not allow things to come into being or pass away. Even so, his answer has serious deficiencies. Unlike Empedocles, Anaxagoras can hold that there really is bone, wood, iron, and cheese in the world. Neither of them, however, can produce a good account of the status of *individual things*.

The world they were trying to account for contains not only a variety of stuffs but also individual objects. Not only bone exists, but also individual bones: a bone is not just a heap of bone stuff. There is not only flesh, hair, blood, and so on, but also particular people and individual pigs, all of which are something more than a *mixture* of those constituents.

Although Empedocles talked about single entities (such as the sun, plants, animals) and although the generation and destruction of such entities form part of his story of the history and future of the cosmos, they cannot, in his theory, really *be*. His theory has room only for speaking of them as mixtures.

Although more (kinds) of things exist in his universe than Empedocles' philosophy allowed, Anaxagoras clearly does not want to say that the sun, Rover, and his own book are uncreated and imperishable. Hence, his system has no place for them as beings, as things that are. They must be treated, quite oddly, as mixtures.

Both Empedocles and Anaxagoras focused on how to apply the Eleatic principle to different kinds of matter and did not see their way to think through the further issues about how particular objects would have to be understood. (The answer would have led them toward the Pythagorean idea of *forms*—a dog or a chair has to do with organization, and not merely with the types of stuff that constitute it.)

Generalizing from Nutrition

Anaxagoras noticed that animals grow by eating. That is, by eating one builds bones, teeth, muscle, hair, and so on. Normally, we think that bread and milk are converted into those substances by metabolic processes. Anaxagoras' Eleatic principles would not, however, allow such comings to be and such destructions as milk being transformed into muscle. "How could hair come from not hair, and flesh from not flesh?" (Fragment 10). Anaxagoras concluded that all these different kinds of stuff must be in the bread, in the milk, in whatever provides nourishment.

He proceeds to make a vast speculative leap from the nutrition case: "In everything there is a portion of everything . . ." (Fragment 11). Not only is hair in bread, but bread is in hair. So too for everything else: any portion of any stuff contains portions of all other stuffs.

Why did he think that larger thesis justified? Presumably because he thought that in the endless sequence of mixtures and separations that constitutes natural "change," what was once one stuff (such as flesh) would be recycled into some other kind of thing (soap, for example). Hence, what was once, say, flesh, must have contained the resultant stuff all along.

Having sketched out that thesis, it might now be obvious how complex his theory of matter is and why commentators, ancient and modern, have found endless fascination in trying to understand its details. I shall briefly mention three of the problems the theory creates.

The simplest problem is this: if bone, for instance, always contains portions of everything else, then why is it bone? The only reasonable answer is that it contains *more* bone stuff than other stuffs. Anaxagoras, like Empedocles, assumes that the proportions in the mixture determine the character of the hunk of matter. It is unlikely that he was interested in providing formulas, however. All he employs is the idea that the stuff most represented in a mixture determines its properties.

The Infinitely Small

How could there be a portion of *everything* in everything? Suppose you took a slice of bone ever so small. How could *that* include an indefinitely large, perhaps infinitely large, number of other stuffs? Anaxagoras had thought of that and has an answer: "Of what is small there is no smallest— there is always a smaller (for it is impossible that what is should cease to be . . .)" (Fragment 3).

He is assuming that matter is continually divisible into smaller pieces. He seems to have thought that if it weren't, at some point in the cutting process the matter would disappear. But that would be to make "what is," the matter, cease to be, and that is impossible. Hence, for any size piece of stuff, there can be smaller pieces. Therefore, no problem arises about, say, an ever-so-small piece of bone containing even smaller portions of everything else, because those other stuffs would be in it in even smaller portions.

In this discussion of the infinitely small, Anaxagoras is most likely carrying on an argument with Zeno, who was also concerned with issues surrounding the question of infinitely small magnitudes.

The Structure of Matter

Anaxagoras construed the things we encounter as mixtures. But does a bone (a mixture) consist of (1) a large number of very small pieces of *pure* bone and (2) lesser numbers of very small pieces of all the other stuffs in a pure state? That is, even though a stuff can be divided smaller and smaller, is there a *naturally* occurring smallest piece of the pure stuff? Or do the portions come in some other way? The following analogy (from Jonathan Barnes) beautifully illustrates the issue:

> A rough analogy may help. Artists may make a patch of their canvas seem green in either of two ways. First, and unusually, that may adopt a *pointilliste* technique, setting minute dots of blue next to minute dots of yellow: from a distance the effect is green; from close up we see adjacent spots of blue and yellow. Alternatively, they may mix masses of blue and yellow on their palette and apply the mixture to the canvas: the effect from a distance is green; and however closely we look at it, the effect is still green. No part of the canvas, however small, is painted blue; and no part yellow. For all that, the green on the canvas "contains" blue and yellow; they are its constituents, and some chemical technique might, for all I know, be capable of "extracting" some of the yellow from the artist's green. (Barnes, 1979, Vol. 2, pp. 23–24)

How did Anaxagoras conceive of his mixtures: are they the result of the combination of small natural bits of matter, or are they a blend? If he seriously meant that in *everything* there is something of everything else, then there could be no pieces of *pure* stuffs. And if there are no pure pieces of anything, then everything is a blend. (The Atomists develop the other, the *pointilliste* answer, that matter is composed of "dots.")

Anaxagoras' Cosmogony

In the beginning, Anaxagoras held, all those stuffs were blended together with absolute uniformity so that the mass of matter had no discernible qualities. (It was thus analogous to the Eleatic One, which had no qualities at all.) Initially, the universal mixture was immobile, but a time came when a rotary motion began in it. As the circulation picked up speed, different stuffs separated off, which meant (since there is no pure stuff) that some kinds of stuffs began to predominate over others in local mixtures. The entire process is as if a blender could be run backward, separating out the ingredients from an original well-mixed concoction.

This appeal to an original unity from which a differentiated cosmos is created by a vortex motion was certainly not new with Anaxagoras. The various elements in the scheme are standard Ionian fare, going all the way back to Anaximander. Generally speaking, in both his cosmogony and in the details of his science that follow from it, Anaxagoras should be understood as bringing the Ionian tradition up to date by adapting it to the changed circumstances caused by the Eleatics.

Mind

Why did the stuffs making up the originally motionless chaos begin to swirl? Just such a question, a request for an *explanation* of change, is characteristic of post-Parmenidean cosmology. Empedocles had invoked notions of love and strife to account for motion. Anaxagoras said that the causal agent was *nous*, "mind."

This notion was not wildly original on Anaxagoras' part. In one sense, he was once again merely carrying on the Ionian tradition. Both Anaximander and Heraclitus had thought of the cosmos as steered by an internal intelligence (and no doubt even that was but a subtle form of ancient anthropomorphism). What Anaxagoras did was, first, make *explicit* the assumption that the cosmos contains such a causal agency and, second, attempt to sharply distinguish between that which steers (causes) and that which is steered (effects).

But what sort of thing is that which runs the cosmos? That is, what is mind? It is in connection with issues about the nature of mind that Anaxagoras struggles. On the one hand, it is clear that he thinks of *nous* as a kind of stuff. However, for Anaxagoras it is a very special stuff, "the finest and purest of all things" (Fragment 12); unlike matter, it is not a mixture of everything else. Now some scholars will hold that because Anaxagoras treats mind as a kind of stuff, even if a uniquely special kind of stuff, it follows that he did not make any interesting progress in sorting out the difference between mind and matter (see Barnes for such an interpretation). Others, such as Guthrie, think it a great achievement for Anaxagoras to have conceived there to be a large difference between mind and other stuffs, while admitting that he was not able to describe the difference as sharply as desired since the philosophical tools necessary to doing so had not yet been fashioned.

Teleology

One discussion that Anaxagoras did stimulate concerned the notion of teleology. (*Telos* is a Greek word meaning "end" or "aim," that is, what is to be accomplished by doing something.) In thinking that the universe is governed by a *logos*, a built-in rationality, Anaximander and Heraclitus had meant by that that the cosmos is *morally* governed. What happens, cosmically speaking, is done for a *telos*, namely for "what is best." So something is *aimed at* in the universe, namely "what is good." Such a view is called *teleological*.

Anaxagoras, in saying that mind is the cause of an organized world, could be taken as implying that cosmological development is for the best. Not only would the tradition he inherited sanction that reading of his words, but so too would an ordinary understanding of what it means to explain a human action by appealing to mind. To say, "He got out of the water because he had a mind to," is to explain the behavior as what the person took to be best, preferable.

Yet Anaxagoras disappointed his teleologically inclined successors. Socrates, Plato, and Aristotle all criticized the way Anaxagoras employed the notion of mind in his cosmological explanations. For although he said that mind stirred the initially immobile mixture into action, he made no use of the notion of mind in explaining any further pieces of natural activity. Subsequent events were explained *mechanically*, that is, without reference to intelligence or to the good. He was, thus, the source of inspiration to both sides in the ensuing dispute: the teleologists and the mechanists could each find their views employed somewhere in Anaxagoras' account.

ATOMISM

The last of the three great post-Parmenidean cosmological systems is called Atomism. Here two men must be considered.

The founder of the system was a person about whom little is known, Leucippus. He was an Ionian Greek, perhaps from Miletus, born sometime before 460 B.C.E. (date of death unknown). He is said to have written two books, of which but a single sentence survives.

He was also the teacher of Democritus, who became the great expositor of Atomism. It is odd to call Democritus a *Pre-Socratic*, as we do: he was born about 460, ten years after Socrates, and lived perhaps thirty to forty years longer than Socrates, who died in 399 B.C.E. He came from Abdera, a provincial *polis* in the northeast. (As shall be seen in the next chapter, Democritus was not the first important intellect to come from Abdera.) Democritus was a professional student who traveled widely in Greece, Egypt, Babylonia, Persia, studying wherever he went. A fragment that may be genuine (Fragment 299) says, "I have travelled more than any man of my time, making the most extensive inquiries, seeing more climes and countries, hearing more learned men. . . ."

Moreover, he was a prolific writer: over fifty books were attributed to him. All have vanished. Although a large number of fragments remain (many themselves extremely fragmentary), those remains are but a miserably small percentage of his total writings:

> Even allowing for the intrusion of some spurious titles, the total is impressive both in amount and in scope, and puts him in a different class from any of his predecessors. It includes treatises on theory of substance (physis), cosmology, astronomy, geography, physiology, medicine, sensation, epistemology, mathematics, magnetism, botany, musical theory, linguistics, agriculture, painting . . . and other topics. (Guthrie, 1965, Vol. 2, p. 388)

At some time and place, Democritus came on Leucippus and adopted his account of nature. Democritus expanded, developed, and more widely applied the scheme originally sketched out by Leucippus. There's not much point in trying to sort out which man contributed what to the fundamentals of the system. Hence they are usually grouped together as the Atomists (or fifth-century Atomists, to distinguish them from their descendants).

Responding to the Eleatics: The Void

Recall that Parmenides assumed that "what is" is stuff, matter. In consequence, he and his followers had held that empty space would be "what is not" and is therefore impossible. Since there cannot be a *void* (to use Melissus' word), the universe must be completely full.

Empedocles and Anaxagoras found no way to criticize that Eleatic thesis. Their cosmic systems thus had no empty space through which things could move. The only form of motion thereby available for use in their theories was the traditional vortex, a swirling of the matter that completely filled space.

The most basic Atomist insight was that the Eleatic denial of void could be criticized. Parmenides had not *argued* that "what is" is identical with matter; he had only *assumed* it. The Atomists simply rejected that assumption and replaced it with the idea that something could exist that is not a stuff— namely, empty space. (They paid a price: they thereby violated the Eleatic thesis that "what is" is homogeneous, *all alike*.)

That done, the Atomists could assert one of their major claims, namely, that *empty space* exists as a cosmic constituent.

They put that thesis paradoxically, however. They said that "not-being" (empty space) exists as well as "being" (matter). That is a striking way of saying that void, which was called "not-being" by their predecessors, is (has being) as much as what the tradition counted as "being," namely matter. (Compare: Modern physicists say that antimatter exists as well as matter. But antimatter *is* matter, though it has characteristics quite different from matter as traditionally described.)

The Atomists' recognition that not everything we can talk about must be theoretically conceived of as matter was a landmark intellectual breakthrough with momentous consequences for philosophy. Although the Atomists themselves did not exploit the realization further than to give themselves the right to talk to empty space, philosophers from Plato on could treat numbers, minds, and gods (and other things, too) as *nonmaterial* items in their metaphysical inventory of what there is.

Particles

In their conception of the material aspect of the world, the Atomists stand in sharp contrast with their predecessors.

Both Empedocles and Anaxagoras held the universe to be composed of kinds of stuffs, elementary forms of matter that differ in their properties and characteristics (water, for example, is fluid and colorless; bone is hard and white). They disagreed about how many fundamental substances there are. The Atomists, however, took the basic material components to be, not stuffs, but *hunks* of matter with no differences between them other than size and shape.

The matter theories of Empedocles and Anaxagoras, on the other hand, represent a *chemical conception of matter.* Their views are forerunners of the modern periodic table with its idea that matter is constituted by a number of elements that combine in various proportions to form nonelementary stuffs.

The Atomists, on the other hand, regarded matter more or less as modern physicists do, that is, as composed of *particles.* The Atomists held the world to be composed of an infinite number of these corpuscles of matter scattered in an infinite space.

Just as other post-Parmenidean cosmologists, the Atomists made no attempt to deal with the Eleatic argument for monism. That conclusion was rejected out of hand, and a number of ultimate (material) things assumed. With respect to space, Leucippus and Democritus agreed with Melissus that Parmenides was wrong in holding that "what is" is spatially limited. On the contrary, space must be unlimited, infinite.

The Atomists' account of individual corpuscles tailored them to be as much like the Eleatic One as possible (except, of course, that many such pieces of being exist). Particles are uncreated and imperishable. They have no characteristics or properties except for a shape and a size. They are usually thought of as very small, too small to perceive, though they differ in size. And they comprise an infinite variety of shapes. Other than in size and shape, they are, as Parmenides said of the One, "all alike."

The particles in themselves cannot change, since they have no qualities. In particular, they cannot be divided (chipped, sliced, worn down, and so on). Division is impossible because no empty space exists inside them. In that respect, they are "completely full," without any *internal* empty space— once again, almost miniature copies of the Eleatic One.

Anaxagoras had held that stuffs are infinitely divisible. The Atomists denied that, asserting on the contrary a natural limit to how far matter can be broken down. Any physical division of matter ultimately results in an indivisible entity. That indivisibility gave the particles their usual name and the system its name: *atomos* meant "indivisible."

The only change these corpuscles (atoms) can undergo is change of place. They can move around in the vast empty space in which they are located.

Motion

Parmenides could have argued that motion is impossible on the grounds that for a thing to change place would mean that it is here and then is not here and, as that would be a transition from being to not-being, changing place is impossible. But his explicit objection to motion rested on the impossibility of void: motion cannot be, because no empty space exists into which a thing could move.

The Atomists, asserting that empty space exists, held that particles move through that void with an infinite variety of motions. But why *should* atoms move? Empedocles and Anaxagoras found it necessary to postulate agencies, love-strife and mind, which stirred the stuffs around to create and destroy new types of matter and new individual objects.

What did the Atomists resort to in their explanation of motion? Basically nothing. They seem to have regarded the motion of atoms in the void as a *fundamental fact* of the universe, no more requiring an explanation than does the existence of matter. To claim that motion is a *given* was not to agree with the original physicists that the stuff of the world undergoes self-initiated change. That view assumes that the cosmic stuff is alive, and most definitely atoms are not living agents. For the Atomists, the original motion is not to be explained *at all*, not even in terms of being self-initiated, self-caused.

Although the initial motion of the particles does not have to be accounted for, present motion is to be explained as the consequence of particles bumping together in their original movements, and rebounding from the collisions, leading to more collisions, and so forth.

World Orders

As the particles, infinite in number and scattered randomly throughout infinite space, move aimlessly in infinite time, every now and again some quantity of them aggregate, cluster. Because atoms come in every conceivable shape, they do not always rebound from the collisions. In jostling about, some become entangled, stuck together in various groupings. A larger pattern of motion ensues (a vortex, in fact), which draws more and more atoms together. Thus a world order comes into being. Eventually, that temporary arrangement of atoms breaks up, and its constituent particles go on their own way into the infinity of space.

As did much of the cosmological tradition, the Atomists countenanced a sequence of worlds. However, they also held that organized worlds *coexist* in the infinity of space. Nor must each cosmos be alike: since they come into being without being planned, an infinite variety of cosmic organizations ensues.

Within any given cosmos—ours, for example—individual objects come into being and pass away in just the same fashion as does a cosmos as a whole. That is, an individual thing is the result of the bumping about of particles and is composed of some of those that have become enmeshed. The individual clump of particles is temporary, continually losing some constituent particles and gaining others until such time as the conglomerate completely breaks down into its elementary bodies.

The Atomists, Leucippus in particular, may have said that these created beings are only appearances, not real beings. That would be either a perfunctory nod to the Eleatics or a misguided way of distinguishing between temporary beings and the everlasting beings (atoms) out of which they are constructed.

A Mechanical World

The Milesians had begun the project of demythologizing the world. But the cosmologists from Thales to Anaxagoras had taken the universe to be a rational arrangement. They *assumed* that even if personal beings are not the cause of natural events, the universe contains a divine being that is the source of the orderly behavior of the cosmos. That agent may be the stuff from which the world is constructed, or it may be some force external to the matter; in either case, a world and its objects not only exhibit intelligence but also conform to moral standards. (The Eleatics, especially Melissus, did not share those assumptions.)

The Atomists denied that entire conception. What comes to be comes to be not by desire or rational planning or for some good purpose. The formation and dissolution of worlds and of their constituent objects is a completely *mechanical* process.

This was the final step in creating a nonanthropomorphic view of the universe. The Atomists' realization that order need not be the result of design, of purposive action, that it can arise mechanically, has become a major theme in Western thought, both ancient and modern.

The Properties of Created Bodies

The objects brought into being by the mindless banging and conjoining of atoms differ from each other in many respects. But how can that be, when their constituent particles are alike except in size and shape?

Individual objects are perceptible while their component atoms are not because they are aggregations of large numbers of minute particles. One object may be heavier than another because it contains less void between its atomic components than the other. The difference between hard things and soft things can also be thus explained.

The atomistic theory of matter differs from its predecessors in not making *substances* basic—stuffs such as earth, air, and blood. Matter was said to consist of extremely small individual objects. How can an Atomist account for the difference between, for example, fire and water, or bread and milk? Any given substance is a congregation of particles of the same size and shape, perhaps having a like arrangement of those atoms. (Fire was said to be composed of very small, very round particles.)

In the atomic theory, the only properties an individual particle has are size and shape. That is, no single atom has a color, taste, texture, or odor. A being created out of atoms also will have a size and shape and may well be large enough to be perceptible. But such perceptible objects also have other properties: those odors, colors, and so on that the single atoms lacked. Or so it seems.

Leucippus and Democritus denied that clumps of atoms have these additional qualities that the individual particles lack. The color, odor, texture, and so on of a thing are not part of the world but are a result of the interaction of the object with a perceiver. Because the atoms of an object affect our sensory organs in certain ways, we experience colors and so on. We attribute those properties to the object, but created beings, just like single atoms, are actually neither hot nor cold, not red or green or blue. "Sweet and bitter, hot and cold, are by convention; by convention is color; in truth there are atoms and the void" (Democritus, Fragment 9).

The Atomists' doctrine that in reality objects have only spatial properties became significant in the modern era in philosophy and science after being reintroduced by Galileo and Descartes. The seventeenth-century terminology spoke of size and shape as "primary properties" and of color, texture, odor, and so on as "secondary properties."

Notice that the distinction between primary and secondary qualities enables the Atomists to satisfy one of Parmenides' specifications about the character of "what is." He had argued that "what is" has no qualities, although when he comes to assume that "what is" is material entity, he gives it spatial properties: "what is" has a size (large, no doubt) and a shape (spherical). All other properties are mere appearance. The Atomists, given their distinction, can also say that things, whether uncreated or created, have no characteristics except spatial ones and that other properties are appearances resulting from the action of particles on sense organs.

Knowledge
The Eleatics were as confident as their predecessors, except for Xenophanes, that it is possible to come to know how things really are. What made them unusual was that they held that reason alone is capable of discovering the nature of things and what reason tells us about reality is not at all what would be expected on the basis of sensory experience.

Empedocles and Anaxagoras, of course, cannot accept that view of the role of the senses in attaining knowledge. Not only does it seem absurd on its face, but it is thoroughly antiscientific. Science aims at explaining phenomena, not at writing them off as mere appearances. They saw, as had Anaximenes long before, that the intellectual aim of science is to make good inferences from the phenomena to an explanation. Still, they could accomplish little beyond the reassertion of that truth.

The Atomists, Democritus in particular, made a more substantial effort to legitimate knowledge. That attempt, however, ended up, as Democritus realized, in contradiction.

First, he too recognized that the scientific project is to make inferences from the phenomena, from what is known of the world via the senses, to an account of what produces those experienced patterns. That is, the senses provide the *evidence* for rational claims about underlying reality. (For example, "An egg, as we can all tell from our senses, is not as solid as a rock of the same size; therefore, there must be more void in the egg than in the rock.")

That line of argument was seconded by Democritus' psychology in which *thought,* the action of the mind, is a form of motion of some of our constituent particles, motion that is caused by changes in the particles making up our sensory organs. In short, thinking is totally dependent on what happens to our senses and has no independent activity.

That the Atomists' thesis about the fundamental reliance of knowledge on the senses came into conflict with another part of their theory made the having of perceptual knowledge impossible. Particles, the basic items of reality, are too small to be perceived individually. We, therefore, cannot perceive the properties atoms *do* have, namely, size and shape. Moreover, what we can detect by our senses—color, texture, and so on—is not really part of the objective world. Thus, all we can tell about the world perceptually is how things appear to us.

Obviously, then, if the senses give us only appearance, any genuine knowledge of how things really are—that is, knowledge that the world is composed of atoms moving in the void—must be attained by reason. Yet the theory of thought mentioned earlier had made any rational understanding of the world depend wholly on the senses. Democritus recognized that the two wings of the theory were in conflict. Fragment 125 records this conflict: He has the Senses complain to the Intellect: "Wretched Mind! You get your evidence from us and then try to overthrow us. If you succeed, you would fail." As a result of that impasse, Democritus was frequently given to skepticism: ". . . in truth we know nothing about anything . . ." (Fragment 7).

Psychology

The philosophical predecessors of the Atomists generally thought of the *psyché* (often vaguely) as a special kind of stuff that continued to exist as an entity with psychological characteristics after the death of the human being (or other animal). The Atomists agreed that there was a special *psyché* stuff, a certain kind of atom, which is only to say a certain size and shape of atom went into the making of a *psyché*. But they held that no individual particle had the ability to animate a body, to be rational, to have a set of memories, thoughts, and so on that constitute a personal identity. An atom, after all, has only a shape and a size. A soul, therefore, must be the result of the interconnection of a number of *psyché* particles in a created being.

That conception of the *psyché's* organization means that on death and dissolution of the living being, the *psyché* itself will also be broken down into its constituent pieces and those scattered with the other particles. Hence there is no such thing as personal survival after death.

Because the earlier Pre-Socratics had not realized that it is possible to make a distinction between material and nonmaterial things, they cannot legitimately be called "materialists." That distinction was clear enough to the Atomists, however, and they clearly *are* materialists. (To achieve that materialism, they must ignore their own recognition of space as a nonmaterial constituent of the cosmos.) They attempted to produce a materialistic explanation for several psychological phenomena: sensation and thinking, along with life and death. After them, a wholly new set of problems came to exist in philosophy: the *mind-body* problem—questions about the nature of soul and mind and about the relationship between the mental and the physical.

The Scientific Program
The Atomists had inherited the ideal originated by Anaximander and so themselves aimed at giving a complete scientific history and description of the world. Thus are found in the Atomists' writings all the scientific topics that had been considered by the tradition over the course of its development: astronomy, geology, meteorology, biology, physiology, medicine. Democritus also made contributions to mathematics.

Little of what they had to say on these matters was original. Most of their work was an attempt to show how such matters *could* be explained on atomistic principles.

Although the cosmological tradition had an evolutionary view of the cosmos and of the origin of human life, by and large their interests were in what we think of as the natural sciences. To a considerable extent, their inquiries did not extend into the social life of human beings. Democritus was a major exception. His lifetime extended well into the succeeding period of philosophy, when philosophers' interests shifted from nature to society. Given the interests of those around him and his own appetite for inquiry, it was entirely natural that he too should have written on topics that his predecessors had not included within the scope of their theorizing.

Thus we find that Democritus carried the evolutionary account of human life into an evolutionary theory of human society (a view common in intellectual circles in the fifth century B.C.E.). He wrote treatises on language and its origin, on social arts such as music and literature. Many of his fragments concern ethics, moral behavior, and even political theory.

The Influence of Atomism
Despite Democritus' catholic intellectual concerns, Atomism was fundamentally a physical theory, drafted in such a way as to have major implications for the question of humanity's place in nature. The theory has been enormously influential.

Both Plato, though he never mentioned Democritus, and Aristotle rejected Atomism: chiefly because they were teleologists and the atomistic view was determinedly mechanistic and materialist.

But those features were attractive in the Hellenistic period of the ancient world and on into the Roman era. One of the major post-Aristotelian philosophical systems was Epicureanism, named for its founder, Epicurus (341–270 B.C.E.). As the background to his moral and religious teaching, he adopted the Atomist physical theory because of its materialism. He did modify the mechanistic aspect: atoms were capable of *some* internally initiated changes of direction.

Later, a Roman poet, Lucretius (99–59 B.C.E.), wrote the major Epicurean work, *De Rerum Natura* ("On the Nature of Things"), a long application of atomistic principles to the natural world. (Anyone interested in seeing how ancient Atomism was made to work should read Lucretius.)

As we all know, modern science accepts Atomism as the correct physical theory. Of course, the *reasons* for its modern acceptance, and the details of the doctrine, differ radically from what was involved in the ancient theory. (What the modern theory calls "atoms," we have learned, are not indivisible. They can be split, though with explosive consequences.) In fundamental respects, modern Atomism is thus greatly different from its ancient counterpart. Nonetheless, the modern idea that matter is particulate was born amid the seventeenth-century rediscovery of ancient Atomism. For that reason, the ancient version was one source of the modern theory.

THE END OF
PRE-SOCRATIC
PHILOSOPHY

The intellectual development we have been studying came to an end. Democritus was the last major figure.

Philosophy did not come to an end, of course. During the course of the fifth century B.C.E., Greek thinkers lost interest in speculating about the history and constitution of the natural world. New intellectual interests and problems arose in place of that original set of issues. Speculation began about human nature and about human behavior in society. To pursue the history of ancient philosophy from this point onward is to put aside the lines of thought we have been examining and to take up a new set of problems.

A THIRD RESPONSE TO PARMENIDES

Clearly, the major explanation for the changing emphasis in philosophy during the fifth century B.C.E. is that inquiries into the history and constitution of the social world came to seem more urgent than similar inquiries into the natural world. Behind that altered perception of priorities were changes in Greek society.

But more was involved. The old problems were not merely abandoned, as a child loses interest in one toy and takes up another. Part of the reason philosophers were led away from the original line of philosophical development was connected with another type of response to Parmenides.

Some few had come to the defense of Parmenides. Others shifted traditional ground as little as possible but as much as seemed necessary to produce cosmological schemes that would satisfy Eleatic arguments. But it was also possible to take even more creative steps in dealing with Parmenides. Here the chief players were Gorgias *(Gor'-ghee-as)* and Protagoras *(Pro-tag'-or -as)*. These two, along with Socrates, were the major figures in the next phase of Greek philosophy.

The following account of Protagoras and Gorgias is limited to a few comments on how they responded to Parmenides. A more full and appropriate discussion of their views and activities is beyond the aims of this book.

GORGIAS

Gorgias was a Sicilian Greek, said to be a student of Empedocles, though he cannot have been much younger. He is one of the great *rhetoricians* of the fifth century B.C.E., an age in which being able to speak well counted for a great deal. Of interest here is one of his treatises. (The book itself has been lost—we have two different paraphrases of its argument.)

That work had the astonishing title *On Nature or What Is Not*. In it he argued three paradoxical theses: (1) that nothing exists; (2) that even if something is, it is unintelligible; and (3) even if it were intelligible, it would be impossible to communicate it. Moreover, the work has the appearance of an Eleatic tract: it is presented as a piece of hardnosed deductive reasoning.

What are we to make of a work whose title says that the natural world is, in words appropriated from Parmenides, "what is not" and that goes on to argue theses seemingly as wild as those of the Eleatics? Scholars today tend to agree that the work is in some way intended to be a parody of the physicists and of the Eleatics. Still, what is the point of the parody? Did Gorgias believe that he had *proved* those theses? Did he even believe that they are true?

It is most difficult to say what he thought he had accomplished. The best guess is that he did not think that he had proven those theses. Most likely, his aim was to say something on the order of "Eleatic arguments are impressive even though the conclusions are hard to swallow. But it is possible to argue other paradoxical conclusions, such as that nothing exists, and so on, with equal plausibility. Nothing can be proved one way or the other. Argumentation is rhetoric—it produces not truth but persuasion."

In this interpretation of the treatise, Gorgias would be condemning the entire tradition, cosmological and metaphysical, for having assumed that inquiry and argument can arrive at the *truth* about how things are. For Gorgias, a skilled orator can make an *equally* impressive case for *every* position. The aim of intellectual activity is not truth, as his predecessors had mistakenly thought, but *persuasion*. Parmenides caused philosophical worries only because everyone assumed that the point of philosophical argument and inquiry is truth. If that is not assumed, then Parmenides can be seen to be nothing more than a good show (and so too Gorgias' own reply). Good rhetorical performances, where truth is not and cannot be an issue, will not cause intellectual cramps.

The various cosmological schemes created by the physicists should be seen in the same light. They are not to be thought of as right or wrong, but as better or worse argued. Any one of them can be as good as any other if only it is skillfully handled.

PROTAGORAS

Protagoras was about the same age as Zeno and Empedocles and Gorgias. He came from Abdera, the provincial *polis* that thirty years later produced Democritus. He seems to have created the profession of Sophist, a profession that became central to philosophy in the last half of the fifth century B.C.E.

Protagoras' most famous saying was "Of all things, man is the measure—of what is, that it is and of what is not, that it is not" (Fragment 1). These ideas were central to the whole of Protagoras' philosophical thought. I do not intend here to examine its full meaning and ramifications. I shall briefly observe how it applies to the question of Protagoras' relation to Parmenides and thereby to the entire philosophical tradition.

Parmenides had held that "what is" is radically different from how things seem. Protagoras in his central thesis asserts that one cannot make that distinction between how things are and how they seem. His dictum means something like "What *seems* to be so to you *is* so." There is nothing "behind" appearances, as Parmenides and the physicists had imagined. Appearances are all that there are, and therefore are identical with "what is."

Unlike Gorgias, Protagoras does not eliminate truth, but rather *relativizes* it to each and every person. What each of us takes to be true is true. The effect of his position is very much the same as that of Gorgias, however. Truth becomes unimportant if each of our judgments, no matter how contradictory, is equally true. For both philosophers the point and aim of inquiry and argument is not the discovery of what is true, of how things really are. Both Parmenides' metaphysics and the attempts to produce a scientific account of the natural world assumed that one could find out *the* truth. For Protagoras there is no such thing, and so it is pointless to pursue that kind of investigation.

THE EFFECT

Both Gorgias and Protagoras undercut the debate about what to do about Parmenides. They each noted that both the Eleatics and their cosmological opponents shared an assumption: that is is possible to attain the truth about how things are through philosophical activity. Both denied that presumption, Gorgias by giving truth to no one and Protagoras by giving it to everyone.

If they were right—and they were very influential—then there was no point in caring about the debates of the previous philosophers. It thus became possible to surrender the old problems and to seek new issues to philosophize about. Those new issues occupied the philosophers who followed. It is to them and to the Sophists that one must now turn.

INDEX